LOW&
SLOW

THE CULINARY INSTITUTE OF AMERICA®

LOW&

THE ART AND TECHNIQUE OF BRAISING, BBQ, AND SLOW ROASTING

SLOW

ROBERT BRIGGS

PHOTOGRAPHY BY PHIL MANSFIELD

Houghton Mifflin Harcourt
Boston • New York • 2014

THE CULINARY INSTITUTE OF AMERICA
President   Dr. Tim Ryan '77, CMC
Provost   Mark Erickson '77, CMC
Director of Publishing   Nathalie Fischer
Senior Editorial Project Manager   Margaret Wheeler '00
Editorial Assistants   Laura Monroe '12
                                             Shelly Malgee '08

For information about permission to reproduce selections from this book, write to Permissions, Houghton Mifflin Harcourt Publishing Company, 215 Park Avenue South, New York, New York 10003.

www.hmhco.com

Library of Congress Cataloging-in-Publication Data
Briggs, Robert, date, author.
  [Low and slow]
  Low & slow : the art and technique of braising, BBQ, and slow roasting / Robert Briggs ; photography by Phil Mansfield ; the Culinary Institute of America.
      pages cm
  Reprint of: Low and slow. —Hoboken, NJ : Wiley & Sons, 2014.
    Includes index.
  ISBN 978-1-118-10591-7 (hardback)
1. Barbecuing. 2. Braising (Cooking) 3. Roasting (Cooking) 4. Sauces. I. Culinary Institute of America. II. Title. III. Title: Low and slow.
  TX840.B3B744 2014b
  641.7'6 —dc23
                          2013042022

Printed in China

TOP 10 9 8 7 6 5 4 3 2 1

Foreword

While our profession has not recognized it as such with formal codification, "low and slow" cooking is one of the most important and widely used approaches to cooking and is found in cuisines all around the globe—whether you are describing slow-roasted veal shanks cooked on a spit in Bavaria, beef brisket being coddled over a mesquite wood fire at a barbecue joint in the heartland of Texas, or a clay pot pork stew cooking in the coals of a fire in Southeast Asia. It's impossible to not be swept up in the anticipation of eating these works of art. All of these dishes are produced by the cook astutely balancing the application of temperature, time, and moisture to render an otherwise tough cut of meat into a delicious dish. Each of these preparations has typically been treated as a discrete and separate approach to cooking—until now. Chef Briggs brings forward his many years as both a professional chef and a culinary educator in this text, which explores this vast and fascinating topic as a unified discipline worthy of official recognition as a foundational cooking method.

I am excited to see this book come to fruition. While reviewing the text and collection of recipes, I found myself applauding Chef Briggs for being brave enough to put forward this study for consideration within a profession that protects its list of codified methods as being sacrosanct. I also read it feeling a bit sorrowful, as Bob passed away from an unbeatable illness before completing the photography for this project. Sadly, he was unable to experience the collaboration by his colleagues at The Culinary Institute of America, who came together to finish his effort out of their friendship and respect for him, and also based on their belief that he was onto something important—a new understanding of how the limitless world of cooking is associated and can be explained.

Mark V. Erickson, CMC

Acknowledgments

I really learned the codification and science of cooking during my last twenty-five years working in various positions at The Culinary Institute of America. Without that experience and my continued education by my colleagues, this book may not have been possible.

I'd like to thank Dr. Timothy Ryan, CMC, the president of the Institute, for suggesting that I write a book. Without that prodding, I may never have stepped up to the plate. I'm grateful for the consultations early in the book process with Mark Erickson, CMC. These early conversations were helpful in steering me in the right direction for the focus of the book.

I'd like to express my gratitude to my wife, Melissa, who for a year provided brutally honest feedback on the outcome of the recipes. This required consuming copious amount of meat weekly. She has since become a pescatarian.

My daughter, Ashley Ngyuen, who missed her calling as a chef, was undoubtedly instrumental in this book. She had lots of questions and we shared plenty of conversations, disagreements, and teasing each other about the execution of the cooking methods in this book.

Thanks to all my friends, relatives, and dinner guests for the year and a half they allowed me to use them as guinea pigs while verifying the recipes. Many of the recipes had to be tested in full volume and it was great to have hungry diners participate, provide feedback, drink a glass of wine or two, and enjoy the experience with me.

This book would not be if it were not for the publishing department at The Culinary Institute of America. It was a pleasure working with Nathalie Fisher and her cheerful personality. Nathalie worked on the proposal with me and navigated through the process to get the project approved.

Maggie Wheeler and Shelly Malgee, also from the publishing department, guided me through every step of the process. Their assistance and guidance was critical in terms of editing, layout, photography suggestions, and answering all of my questions during the process.

My oncologist Dr. Abraham Mittleman and surgeon Dr. Beth Schrope deserve credit for the completion of this book. Without their expertise and care, this book may have never come to fruition.

Finally, I would like to thank Weber-Stephen Products LLC for generously donating the equipment that was used in the recipe testing and photography for this book. We could not have completed this project without their help. To learn more about Weber's line of products, see their website at www.weber.com or call 1-800-GRILLOUT.

Introduction

The seed for this book started with the purchase of my first kettle charcoal grill. After producing some mediocre, over-smoked, and undercooked barbecued meats, I was driven to learn more about the process. I began doing extensive research and practicing my barbecuing and smoking skills at home. As a professional chef, when I think of cooking a less tender cut of meat, braising is the first cooking process that comes to mind, but eventually I connected the dots and realized that barbecuing and slow roasting also provide the same outcome. They make tougher, underutilized, deeply flavored cuts of meats tender and exceptionally flavorful by employing low levels of heat and long cooking times.

I've developed these recipes utilizing my forty years of cooking experience at home and in professional kitchens. I have also taught hundreds of home cooks to prepare less tender cuts of meat using these low and slow cooking techniques in Adult Education classes at The Culinary Institute of America. Although I have included plenty of recipes for side dishes to accompany the main dishes, the primary objective of this book is to explain the cooking techniques that can be used to tenderize tougher cuts of meat. Pork shoulder, beef brisket, spareribs, and shanks are all tough cuts of meat that

become not only palatable but delicious when cooked using the three basic techniques demonstrated in this book. There are no preservatives or additives such as nitrates, nitrites, or food colorings used in the recipes, and all of the ingredients are available in most supermarkets, although you may occasionally need to make a special request from the meat cutter or butcher.

Although certain cooking techniques tend to be associated with specific seasons of the year, the selection of recipes and techniques in this book are designed to be used year-round. Obviously the roots of barbecue are firmly planted as an outdoor cooking method, so the barbecue recipes naturally lend themselves to be used in the summer months—it doesn't get much better than enjoying barbecue outdoors on a warm summer day. Call me crazy, but I don't limit barbecuing to only summertime. Several times a winter I'll shovel the snow from around my barbecue, fire it up, and wrap it in insulating blankets, and enjoy some ribs, brisket, or pork butt.

Unlike barbecuing, braising is an indoor technique that tends to be used more in the winter. In the cooler months it makes sense to cook something hearty in the oven for an extended period of time while the aroma of comfort food wafts through the house. Although the cooking time can be lengthy, the attention the food actually requires is minimal, and it's a one-pot meal so even the cleanup is easier.

Slow roasting is a year-round cooking technique that bridges the gap. It utilizes a long, slow cooking process like braising, but it is a dry heat cooking method like barbecuing. Slow roasting can be done outdoors by slow cooking a pork roast on a grill, or indoors by slowly roasting a comfort food like lamb shoulder in an oven.

It is most important to understand the three cooking processes. Each process is explained in detail at the beginning of its chapter, and once you've mastered the technique, you can apply it to different types of meat and create hundreds of new dishes. Making changes to a recipe may require some minor alterations, like the lengthening or shortening the cooking times or using a larger or smaller pot, but the general technique will remain the same. You can also personalize your creations by experimenting with seasonings to create different flavor profiles and matching your main course with some of the accompaniments in the book for a complete meal.

1 GETTING STARTED

Low and slow techniques have been used since cooking began. Prehistoric man discovered that cooked meat was easier to chew, more palatable, and safer: Cooking kills germs and parasites in raw meat, and consequently prevents illness and death. Some theories suggest the reason we're not extinct is because we learned how to cook. For thousands of years, man cooked his meat near an open fire using direct heat. Over time, this way of cooking evolved to use indirect heat.

What Is Low and Slow Cooking?

THE PRECURSORS TO MODERN OVENS were no more than pits dug into the ground, with heat generated either by a fire or by hot rocks. Food was placed directly in the pits to be roasted. When early man learned to create pottery, pits gave way to clay ovens. Eventually, the fire moved inside the home, with open hearths, and was used for direct cooking (meat could be roasted on skewers) and indirect cooking (food could be simmered in a cauldron). Over time, these cooking methods were refined into the way we cook today.

The concept of low and slow cooking refers to cooking meat over a low temperature—generally between 185° and 250°F, depending on the process—for a long period of time. Cooking in this manner tenderizes otherwise tough cuts of meat. This book focuses on the three low and slow techniques:

Braising Also called "pot roasting," braising is a combination cooking technique in which meat is typically first seared to develop flavor and visual appeal, and then combined with liquid, covered, and cooked very slowly in an oven until the meat becomes tender. The cooking liquid can then be used to make a sauce to serve alongside the meat. Unlike standard roasting, braising uses less tender cuts of meat and makes them palatable.

Barbecuing Much like roasting, barbecuing is a dry-heat method during which either an open flame or the hot air inside an enclosed chamber cooks the meat. It is differentiated from roasting by a much lower cooking temperature and by the application of smoke to the food during cooking for clean added flavor. Less tender cuts of meat are also used.

Slow Roasting This method uses the heat of the oven to cook flavorful, more active, less tender meat at a lower temperature and over a longer period of time than used in standard roasting. The drippings that accumulate at the bottom of the pan are used to make an accompanying sauce.

The recipes at the beginning of each chapter are master recipes that illustrate the key steps of the techniques in the book. They use the same cut of meat in order to demonstrate the differences in each technique.

MEATS FOR LOW AND SLOW COOKING

It is important to understand the types of meat used for low and slow cooking or the results could be drastically different than what is desired. Typically, the tougher and less expensive cuts are preferred for low-and-slow cooking techniques since the cooking process breaks them down and tenderizes them. Meat from different parts of an animal varies greatly depending on the type of muscle and how much it has been exercised. General similarities exist among cuts of beef, veal, lamb, venison, and pork if they come from the same parts of the butchered animal. Muscle sections that are used more frequently or to perform arduous tasks will be tougher than more sedentary muscle groups. Muscles that are located along the back are used less frequently than muscles that are at the extremities. Therefore, the rib and the loin contain the tenderest cuts. They tend to cost more than cuts from the shoulder, which are often more exercised and tougher. The popularity of barbecue has turned pork ribs in particular into the "filet mignon" of pork in terms of price: They are expensive and used almost exclusively for barbecue. The leg may contain tender cuts as well as cuts that are quite tough. The age and method of raising the animal also determine a level of tenderness. What may be considered a quality cut in one species can be quite tough in another. The diagrams shown here are the muscular structures of the cow and the pig and outline where the different cuts of meat come from.

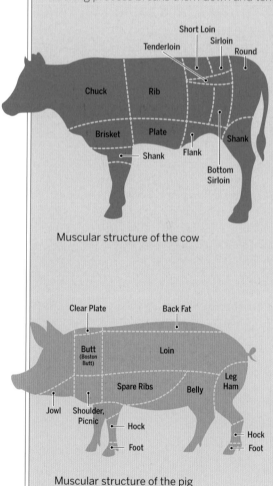

Muscular structure of the cow

Muscular structure of the pig

3

PORK AND BEEF

Two specific cuts of meat that are used frequently in barbecue preparations are beef brisket and pork ribs. Since the brisket is found lower on the cow, it tends to be tough but very flavorful. The brisket has multiple uses. It is a mainstay of beef barbecue, being smoke-roasted for hours. Brisket, cured and seasoned, is used for corned beef and pastrami. It is a favorite as a pot roast as well. They usually weigh 10 to 12 pounds each. Brisket consists of two cuts, the "flat" and the "point." Most of the time, you will want to buy and cook the brisket whole. However, to feed a smaller crowd, you may wish to purchase only part of a brisket. The flat cut is leaner and best used for braising, while the point cut is best for barbecuing. The point cut is a thicker, fattier cut, containing a layer of fat between two muscles; it can be easily identified by its pointy shape. These cuts are usually in the 6-pound range.

Pork spareribs are often known as belly or rack ribs; they are wider and generally meatier than their baby back rib cousin. The full sparerib can be purchased without the brisket bones and trimmed to make a more uniform rib. These are often known as St. Louis ribs and are normally priced slightly higher.

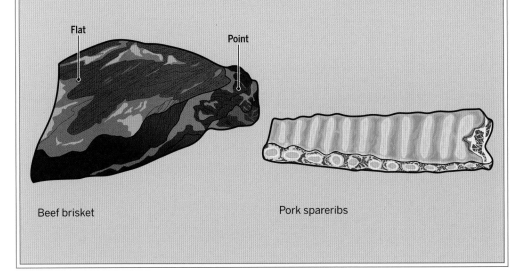

Flat   Point

Beef brisket   Pork spareribs

Tools

HAVING THE CORRECT TOOLS for the job certainly makes cooking easier, and you may already have much of the equipment listed here. The items listed below are those that are needed for the specific techniques in this book; some of the items are more critical than others. You will also need common kitchen tools such as spatulas, wooden spoons, and measuring cups. Think about your specific needs, and plan any equipment purchases accordingly. For example, if you don't plan on making a lot of barbecue, you can get by with a basic gas or charcoal grill; it isn't necessary to pay hundreds or thousands of dollars for a fancy smoker. Also, all of the braised items in this book can be cooked in a large, deep pot with a lid; it isn't necessary to purchase a slow cooker with a lot of bells and whistles. The slow cooker can be more convenient, and that is often what you are paying for with higher-priced or specialty pieces of equipment: convenience. One critical tool, however, is a dual-probe thermometer. Maintaining proper temperatures is very important to all types of slow cooking, and a thermometer with two probes allows you to accurately monitor the temperature inside the cooker as well as the internal temperature of the food for a perfectly cooked product.

BRAISER OR DUTCH OVEN

A braiser, or Dutch oven, is a high-sided round or oval pot with a tight-fitting lid. It is usually made of stainless steel or enameled cast iron. It is meant to be used for braising and stewing on the stovetop and in the oven.

SLOW COOKER

The slow cooker is electric and is used, as the name implies, for slow cooking. Like braisers and Dutch ovens, slow cookers have tight-fitting lids to hold in moisture. They are excellent for the long, slow cooking method of braising because the meat cooks in the liquid at a low temperature, but are not a must-have item, as braising can be easily done in the oven.

GRILLS

A gas grill (pictured below, left) or charcoal grill (pictured below, right) works well for barbecuing, and most homes already have one. You can cook over either direct or indirect heat when using a grill, depending on where you concentrate the heat. Low- and slow-cooked foods are usually cooked over indirect heat: The fire and smoke are concentrated on one side of the grill and the food cooked on the other side. On a charcoal grill, this is controlled by the placement of the coals (see photos, opposite). When using a charcoal grill, a few wood chunks can be placed on top of a few smoldering charcoal chunks to create flavorful smoke. Some gas grills come with a steel firebox that can hold some wood chips

Gas grill

Charcoal grill

Placing the coals in the center of a charcoal grill concentrates the fire for direct cooking.

To create indirect heat on a charcoal grill, move the coals to one side and cook the food on the other side.

and be placed over a gas burner set on low (see photo, right). With any type of grill, the lid is closed and left undisturbed for as long as possible to smoke and cook the food. A thermometer must be used to monitor the chamber temperature so that the heat can be increased or decreased as needed. The heat level is controlled by turning down the heat on a gas grill or by adjusting the vent holes on a charcoal grill.

A smoke box filled with wood chips allows a gas grill to produce fragrant wood smoke.

WIRE BRUSH OR GRILL BRUSH

It is important to keep the grates of your grill clean. Use a long-handled brush with wires at the end to scrub the grill grates and remove any debris or burnt-on material left from previous use. It's best to have a grill brush with a long handle, but don't spend a lot of money on a fancy grill brush or an electric version; they're not worth it.

Just before grilling, brush the hot grill grates vigorously to remove any large particles, then carefully rub the grates with cooking oil on a cloth to remove any finer particles and black soot. Allow the grates to reheat before placing any food on them. This process not only cleans the grates, it also seasons them so that the food is much less likely to stick to the surface.

CHIMNEY CHARCOAL STARTER

A charcoal starter is used to heat charcoal before transferring it to the grill. A few sheets of newspaper are placed in the bottom, and the coal is piled on top.

Once lit, the heat moves upward to ignite the coals. This efficient way of lighting charcoal eliminates the need for lighter fluid. Petroleum-based lighter fluid imparts an undesirable flavor and aroma into the finished product and should never be used.

Chimney charcoal starter

SMOKERS AND BARBECUE PITS

For barbecuing, you need a chamber that will hold the food to be barbecued or smoked and contain the heat and smoke. A dedicated smoker can sometimes be preferable to a grill because it can maintain a more consistent temperature, allows for more airflow control than some grills, and contains a water pan to produce a high-humidity environment that won't dry out the meat. Several kinds are available, and can be as high or low tech as your budget will allow. Some people even make their own smokers by placing a hot plate inside a covered container such as a new trash can or two large stacked planter pots.

Bullet smokers are tall, narrow units topped with a tight-fitting lid, so they look like a large bullet. These units have two racks inside that hold the product above a water pan, which is placed above the fire. A very popular bullet smoker for home use is the Weber Smokey Mountain smoker, or "WSM" as it is called in the barbecue world. It works very well for the home hot smoker or barbecue enthusiast because it is easy to

use. It is composed of durable enameled steel, has a large door that allows you to add fuel and water without removing the lid, and doesn't take up a lot of space.

Ceramic cookers are similar to bullet smokers in many ways, but made of ceramic material. This allows them to attain a much higher heat for grilling and to maintain the heat with a minimum amount of added fuel or smoking material. Less attention is needed with ceramic smokers because they maintain a nice, even heat for a long period of time. One popular ceramic cooker for home cooks is the Big Green Egg. The convenience and quality of the Big Green Egg does come with a hefty price tag, more than twice that of a WSM.

Electric smokers come in a wide variety of shapes, sizes, and prices. These units have a chamber that will hold several racks and space to hang food inside. They also have a water pan to keep the humidity level high. An adjustable electric element that produces heat allows for an even temperature, and there is also an internal or external smoke generator to produce the smoke for the chamber. Electric smokers have a heating element that will smolder wood sawdust, wood chips, or compressed sawdust briquettes that are produced by the manufacturer. This style of smoker can often be set up and let go for hours with little or no attention.

The sky's the limit when it comes to barbecue pits or offset smokers. Barbecue pits are permanent structures that are built expressly for barbecuing meat in the backyard, while an offset smoker offers a bigger chamber than a bullet smoker to hold large quantities of meat. They both can range in cost from a few hundred to tens of thousands of dollars. Offset smokers are made of heavy-gauge cast iron or steel, which makes them very heavy and difficult to move. A special feature of these smokers is that they have a wood chamber that is separate from the cooking chamber. They can range from a backyard smoker purchased at a home improvement center to a smoker that is custom built on a trailer and pulled by an automobile or tractor trailer truck, although the latter is usually reserved for the very serious home cook or professional who will enter competitions or sell barbecue at events.

DRIP PAN

A drip pan is used to collect the fat and juices that drip from the meat during barbecuing or roasting. In roasting these drippings can be used to make a sauce. When barbecuing, the drip pan prevents flare-ups by collecting the dripping fat, and, when water is added, can do double duty as an alternative to a water pan (see below).

WATER PAN

While barbecuing, a metal pan is often filled with water, juice, beer, or other liquid and placed beneath the food as it cooks. This helps to moderate the temperature and provides humidity to the cooking chamber.

THERMOMETERS

A thermometer is an essential piece of equipment when cooking meats. Monitoring the internal temperature of the meat with a thermometer allows you to perfectly cook the meat to a specific

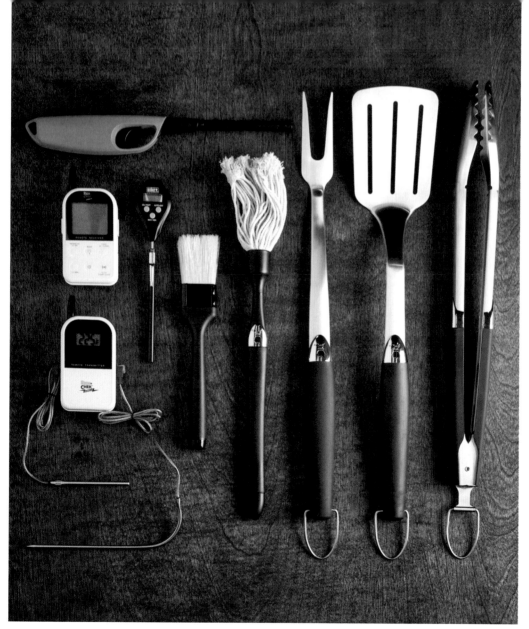

A thermometer is one of the most essential tools for low and slow cooking. A wireless dual-probe version with a remote, pictured at left, is the best option, but you may also use a single-probe thermometer. Other useful hand tools include, from left to right, a lighter, pastry brush, mop brush, kitchen fork, spatula, and tongs.

THE VITAL IMPORTANCE OF THERMOMETERS

Invest in a good-quality and reliable thermometer. The cost of a dry, overcooked, or otherwise ruined pork butt or strip loin of beef is possibly more expensive than the price of the thermometer that could have saved the meal and saved you the embarrassment.

Monitoring temperatures is a critical part of the cooking processes described in this book. I highly recommend that you purchase a dual probe wireless thermometer that includes a transmitter and receiver. The two probes allow you to monitor the meat temperature and the cooking chamber temperature at the same time, and the remote station allows the thermometer to be wherever you are. You can set alarms and monitor the meat temperature without having to lift the cover of the cooking chamber. This may sound like overkill, but these cooking processes require very specific temperatures and a reliable thermometer makes all the difference.

When using any type of meat thermometer, place the probe in the center of the thickest part of the meat. The end of the probe should not be very close to or touching any bones or fat pockets because they can cause an unreliable, inflated temperature reading.

Many ovens and slow cookers have temperature probe options. They are useful for monitoring the meat temperature while braising or roasting. It's recommended that you periodically verify that the actual oven temperature matches the temperature setting using an oven thermometer. To do this, place the thermometer in the oven, preheat the oven to any temperature, and then make sure the temperature reading of the oven matches that of the thermometer. Ideally, they should be within a few degrees of each other.

doneness, as in the case of prime rib, or to determine if the meat, such as a roast chicken, is fully cooked.

A basic dial probe thermometer with a nut on the back of the dial for adjusting calibration is a good choice. They are easy to read, durable, and water resistant and do not need batteries. They are excellent for checking meat temperatures when roasting, braising, or smoking.

A dual probe digital wireless thermometer is a perfect tool for barbecuing, when the temperature of the cooking chamber as well as the internal temperature of the meat should be closely monitored. It's an ideal solution to have one probe inserted into the meat and the other inside the cooking chamber. This type of thermometer also allows you to check the temperature of the chamber and the meat from a distance without having to lift the cover of the cooking chamber.

BRINING NEEDLES

Brining needles are used to pump brine or flavoring ingredients into the center of the meat. The needle is inserted into the meat, and then slowly extracted while pressing on the plunger. You can inject brine directly into the meat to speed up the brining process, or inject the marinade if marinating the exterior alone will not penetrate to the center of a thick piece of meat. A brining needle can be used for all three of the cooking methods in this book. Unless you plan to brine very large pieces of meat regularly, you need only purchase a small, inexpensive brining needle designated for home use.

SPICE GRINDER OR COFFEE GRINDER

Grinding your own whole spices provides much more flavor than using ground or powdered spices from the store. Small quantities can easily be ground using a mortar and pestle. When larger quantities are needed, an electric coffee grinder makes fast work of it and allows for more control over the size of the final grind. The grinder that you use should be dedicated to spices only, because the spices will impart some flavor into the machine.

SPICE SHAKER

Spice shakers are cylinders with perforated holes at the top that you can use for making and storing your own custom rubs. They are the perfect tool for holding spices or dry rub mixtures because they allow for an easy and even application of the contents.

PASTRY BRUSHES

Pastry brushes are available in a variety of sizes and can be used to brush sauce onto barbecued products or to baste roasted foods. A long-handled brush is best in order to keep your hand away from the heat source. Do not purchase pastry brushes with plastic or nylon bristles; they can burn or melt when they touch something hot. I do not recommend silicone brushes either, because silicone does not allow anything to stick to it. When a silicone brush is dipped into a sauce or mop, very little liquid adheres to it, which makes your task take much longer. If possible, purchase brushes that are made from natural boar bristles and that are dishwasher safe. Brushes used for barbecuing can be difficult to get clean, and washing them in a dishwasher is the best way to ensure that they are properly sanitized. Otherwise, brushes must be washed very thoroughly in hot water and sanitizing soap to prevent food-borne illnesses.

If you're only going to buy one brush, a 2-inch brush is good for general purposes. A 1-inch brush is the perfect size for smaller items, and a 3-inch brush is appropriate if you are going to be barbecuing larger items.

MOP BRUSHES

Like small floor mops, mops for barbecuing have long wooden handles with fabric strips attached to one end. They are used to slather, or mop, sauces onto barbecued and slow-roasted foods. Like pastry brushes, wash mop brushes in the dishwasher or clean them very thoroughly in hot water and sanitizing soap after each use. Soaking them in water treated with a little bleach can also sanitize them and help keep the fabric looking whiter.

SPRAY BOTTLE

For moistening foods during the barbecuing process, select a food-grade plastic bottle that can contain and spray a fine mist of liquid. For mops that are thin and do not contain particles (such as herbs or red pepper flakes) it is easier to use a spray bottle than a mop brush, and you will find that a spray bottle wastes much less of the liquid.

SQUIRT BOTTLE

Different from a spray bottle, a squirt bottle is a tall cylindrical bottle with a pointed screw-on top. Store-bought mustard or ketchup squeeze bottles are typical examples and can be washed out and reused for your homemade sauces. Squirt bottles are great for quickly squirting a sauce onto a meat or for basting the meat during the roasting or barbecuing process.

TONGS

Tongs allow the quick turning or removal of large pieces of food from a cooking surface. Long-handled tongs are ideal for grilling or barbecuing, while shorter tongs are useful for the stovetop. You can also purchase locking tongs that save storage space because they are more compact when locked. The downside to locking tongs is that they can be annoying when you need to use them quickly, and you are fumbling around to get them unlocked while an item is burning. Use every type of tongs with care; they can tear up the flesh or skin of a meat or mess up a glaze.

ROASTING PANS

Shallow-sided, rectangular roasting pans allow for free circulation of hot air while roasting in the oven. It is the circulation of the hot air that cooks the roasted food evenly, so it is critical to the roasting process that the sides of the pan not be too tall (not more than 3 or 4 inches). Use a rack that fits in the pan to elevate the food for better air circulation.

When choosing a pan, select one that is the correct size for the meat. It should be large enough that the items inside do not touch the side of the pan or each other, but not too large; in a pan that is too much bigger than the food, the drippings evaporate more quickly and can burn easily, ruining your sauce.

15

KNIVES

These will be used more often than any other set of equipment in your kitchen, so be sure to select high-quality knives that are built to last. Blades of high-carbon stainless steel will take and keep a sharp edge and will not discolor, stain, or rust. Stamped knives are cut from a single sheet of steel. Forged high-carbon stainless-steel knives will be more expensive than stamped knives, but they will also last longer and have better balance.

A basic knife set should include the following:

» Boning knives with narrow, sharply pointed blades offer good maneuverability and are used for separating raw meat cleanly from the bones.

» Slicers with long, narrow, sharp blades, sometimes serrated, are good for cutting even, smooth slices of cooked meat.

» Chef's, or French, knives will be the most used knives in your kitchen. They are used for a wide variety of cutting tasks, from chopping onions to mincing herbs to slicing meats. The sturdy heel of the long, tapered blade can cut through small bones, while the middle of the blade and tip can finely slice and mince items. Select a blade that is 8 to 10 inches long.

» Paring knives, with blades from 2 to 4 inches long, are designed for peeling and trimming vegetables but are good for any finer, more delicate trimming work that may need to be done.

» Steels are used to hone and realign the blades of knives to keep the edge sharper for a longer period of time. They are usually rounded and 10 to 12 inches long. Ceramic and diamond-impregnated steels are also available.

» Kitchen forks are used to test the doneness of meats and vegetables, to lift large items, and to steady meat or poultry while carving.

It's important to keep the blades of your knives sharp and well honed. Sharp knives cut better and are safer to use; the more pressure you need to apply to cut with a dull knife, the more likely the blade is to slip and the more damage it can do if it does. Knives can be professionally sharpened at cutlery stores, but avoid anyone who uses electric grinding stones to sharpen knives; these stones grind away too much of the knife material, which shortens the life of the knife and ruins the blade.

Always use a wooden cutting board; cutting on metal, glass, or marble will dull and damage knife blades.

GLOVES

Plastic and vinyl gloves are good when handling and pulling apart fatty meat products. They help keep the food safe, keep your hands cleaner, and can even help you safely handle a hot product, especially if you layer on two pairs of gloves.

Heavy fireproof gloves are useful for barbecuing. Heavy plastic gloves can be used to remove meat from the smoker and to pull hot meat as well. Leather gloves are even more heat resistant and can be used to handle hot pieces of equipment, such as a charcoal igniter or water pan.

FIRE EXTINGUISHER

If you don't have a fire extinguisher already, you should definitely purchase one and keep it in a handy location. Purchase a fire extinguisher that is approved for most home fires, such as the Kidde 3-A: 40-B:C or a similar Class B type. This type of fire extinguisher will cover most household fires including those involving combustible liquids, such as fat and grease. Always have a fire extinguisher nearby when barbecuing or grilling in case any flare-ups get out of hand. Though deep-frying is not covered in this book, a fire extinguisher is a must when deep-frying large items, such as a whole turkey, outside.

Fuels

You don't need added fuels for cooking on the stovetop, in the oven, or in a slow cooker, of course, but fuel is necessary for barbecuing or for spit-roasting over a flame. As described in the equipment section, some smokers and barbecue pits supply heat to the chamber using electricity or gas, with the smoke generated separately, outside or within the chamber. Others burn charcoal to generate heat. Some grills, pits, and smokers utilize only wood for both heat and smoke, and produce the highest-quality food products. Barbecuing with a wood-fired grill, pit, or smoker takes some time to master, since the size of the fire and the smoky heat is controlled by the airflow that is allowed to reach the fire; the vents need to be carefully adjusted and monitored in order to maintain the optimal temperature of 225° to 250°F with a light flow of smoke. For the recipes in this book, use whichever fuel you prefer.

CHARCOAL

Wood sawdust or scraps of wood that are left over from manufacturing processes are combusted using low oxygen to produce charcoal. This process removes any wood flavor, so the job of charcoal is solely to produce heat. From this basic state, charcoal can take on several forms, including briquettes and lump charcoal. The quality, which varies widely, can greatly impact the flavor and aroma of your final product.

Charcoal Briquettes

Charcoal briquettes were invented in 1920 as a way to utilize the wood scraps that were a by-product of the production of Ford automobiles. Henry Ford came up with the idea to smolder the wood pieces and compress them into briquettes. Ford eventually turned the job of producing charcoal over to his brother-in-law, E. G. Kingsford, and Kingsford remains a leading brand of charcoal today.

A drawback to using briquettes is the other ingredients that are included in the process used to make them. For example, coal is commonly used as a binder, and lime may be added in order to produce the white ash that forms on the charcoal to show when it is hot enough. Petroleum products, which can add a distinctively unpleasant aroma and flavor to the food, may also be included to guarantee quick ignition. Never purchase "quick-start charcoal," which are charcoal briquettes that have

CLOCKWISE FROM LEFT: crumpled newspaper, lump charcoal, and charcoal briquettes.

Different woods impart different flavors into the food with which they are cooked. Pictured clockwise from top: apple wood sawdust, cherry wood sawdust, hickory wood sawdust, oak wood chunks, apple wood chunks, apple wood chips, and alder wood chips.

been pretreated with lighter fluid. Always purchase high-quality charcoal briquettes.

Lump Charcoal

Lump charcoal is carbonized hardwood that is left in its natural shape. It is not compressed into briquettes, eliminating the need for additives and making it a better choice than briquettes. It also ignites easily, burns hotter and cleaner, produces less ash, and provides a steadier flame. The disadvantages of lump charcoal are that it burns faster, so it needs to be added to the fire more frequently, and it is also more expensive than briquettes. However, the advantages far outweigh the disadvantages, making lump charcoal the preferable choice.

WOOD

Smoke is a critical ingredient in the barbecue or smoking process because it provides flavor to the products being cooked. Different woods can produce widely different flavors in the end product (see chart, page 71). Nonresinous hardwoods such as hickory, oak, and maple are used for barbecue, while soft resinous woods such a pine or cedar must be avoided. A general rule of thumb is: If a tree loses its leaves for the winter months, it can be used for barbecuing.

19

2 BRAISING

Braising, barbecuing, and slow roasting are all long, low cooking methods that utilize less tender, fattier cuts of meats with a lot of connective tissue. But braising stands apart in that it includes liquid in the cooking process. It is also a combination cooking method—one that uses both dry and moist heat—and involves cooking in a covered pot, which is why it is also called "pot roasting." This combination of dry and low slow moist heat tenderizes and develops a deep, rich flavor in these less tender cuts of meat.

THE FIRST STEP WHEN BRAISING is the dry heat: searing the meat in a small amount of hot oil. This browns the outside of the meat and gives the end product a deep, rich flavor. It also causes the meat to release drippings, called the "fond," that caramelize in the bottom of the pot. These drippings in turn add flavor to the sauce.

The second step is the application of moist heat: adding cooking liquid to the pot. The cooking liquid usually consists of a rich broth or stock, a combination of stock and wine, or a combination of stock and another sauce such as brown sauce. Aromatic vegetables, herbs, and other ingredients can be added to the cooking liquid to provide even more flavor. Tomato paste, for example, contributes color, flavor, and some acid to the sauce. During cooking, the liquid will thicken into a rich sauce that can be served alongside the meat.

The sauce is a critical part of the braising process. It provides moisture and flavor to the meat. It can be thickened with a prepared roux or by adding flour to the pan before adding the braising liquid; by puréeing any aromatic vegetables cooked in the sauce; or simply by reducing to the desired consistency. More vegetables, such as carrots, peas, onions, and potatoes, can also be added at the end of the cooking process and cooked in the sauce to make a one-pot meal.

Choose a heavy-gauge braising pot or Dutch oven with a tight-fitting lid, large enough and shaped to hold the meat comfortably. There are oval pots on the market with tight-fitting lids that are developed specifically for this process. Alternatively, you could use a roasting pan covered tightly with aluminum foil. A slow cooker can also be used, but most models require searing the meat in a separate pot or pan. You will need a kitchen fork to remove the meat and to determine "fork-tenderness," meaning that the meat will slip easily from the fork when it is done, and a fine-mesh strainer to strain the sauce when the meat is finished. The meat will need to be sliced with a carving knife.

MASTER TECHNIQUE

Sear meat over high heat before it is braised to give it a deep, rich color and flavor, and then remove the meat from the pot.

Add aromatic vegetables and herbs to the fond for additional flavor.

THE SCIENCE BEHIND SEARING

While it is a common belief that searing will seal the outside of the meat and help to retain the juices, this is a myth. Searing does not seal in juices; it provides flavor and color to the meat and sauce. To properly sear a cut of meat, cook it over high heat until browned. Do not overload the pan or pot, or the meat will steam or boil, and will not develop the desired color and flavor. A side benefit of searing is that you will develop a fond in the pan, which contributes to the flavor of the sauce. Always check the fond in the pan for taste before proceeding with the rest of the recipe. If the fond is burnt and you taste any slight bitterness, discard it and make the sauce without it. It's better to go without it than to add bitterness to the sauce.

3.

If desired, incorporate tomato paste to give a braised dish color and add a bit of acid to help balance the flavors.

4.

Return the seared meat to the pot.

5.

Pour the prepared sauce or braising liquid over the meat.

6.

Thicken the cooking liquid to the proper consistency and bring it to a gentle simmer before transferring the pot to the oven.

7.

Cover the pot and place it in the oven. The cooking liquid should remain at a gentle simmer throughout the cooking time.

8.

The finished meat should be fork-tender and succulent.

9.

If desired, strain the sauce before serving.

Braised Pulled Pork Barbecue Sandwiches with Coleslaw

Along with ribs and brisket, pulled pork is a staple wherever barbecue is served, from picnics to food trucks to restaurants. Although pulled pork is traditionally smoked, this braised version can be made and enjoyed year-round without any specialty equipment.

SLOW COOKER METHOD

1. Trim most of the external fat from the pork butt.

2. In a pan large enough to hold the pork, heat the oil over medium to high heat. Meanwhile, season the pork with 1 teaspoon of the black pepper and 1 teaspoon of the salt.

3. When the oil is near the smoke point (see Chef's Notes, page 36), add the pork to the pan and sear the meat on all sides. You want to achieve a caramelized, dark brown color while being careful not to burn the drippings in the pan.

4. While the pork is browning, combine the barbecue sauce, apple cider vinegar, brown sugar, red pepper flakes, and the remaining 1 teaspoon black pepper and 1 teaspoon salt in a small bowl.

5. When the pork has been seared on all sides, remove the pan from the heat. Remove the pork from the pan and reserve it, covered with aluminum foil. Pour out and discard all of the fat left in the pan. Deglaze the pan with the water, scraping the fond with a wooden spoon to loosen it from the pan. Taste the drippings; if they taste at all bitter, do not use them.

One 6- to 8-lb pork butt or pork shoulder, bone in

1 tbsp canola oil or corn oil

2 tsp freshly cracked black pepper

2 tsp kosher salt

1⅔ cups Classic Barbecue Sauce (page 216; see Chef's Notes)

½ cup apple cider vinegar

2 tsp packed light brown sugar

½ tsp crushed red pepper flakes

¼ cup water

¼ tsp ground cayenne pepper (see Chef's Notes)

8 soft white hamburger buns, or 16 slices soft white bread

2 cups Coleslaw (page 163)

6. Sprinkle the pork with the cayenne. Place the pork and pan drippings, if using, into the slow cooker and add the barbecue sauce mixture.

7. Set the slow cooker on low and cook the pork, turning occasionally, until the meat slides easily off a fork when punctured, 10 to 12 hours for an 8-pound pork butt. The meat can also be checked with a thermometer; the pork is done when it has reached an internal temperature of 193°F.

8. When the pork has finished cooking, remove the insert from the slow cooker base, and allow the pork and sauce to cool in the covered insert for about 20 minutes.

9. Carefully skim as much fat as possible off of the surface of the sauce. If the sauce is very thick, you can add some water to thin it out. If the sauce is too thin to cling to the meat, slightly reduce it in a pan over medium heat until it reaches the desired consistency.

10. When cool enough to handle, remove the pork from the sauce and pull it into strips using two forks or your fingers. The meat can also be chopped into small ½- to ¾-inch chunks or strands using a knife. If you discover any large pieces of fat while pulling the meat, remove and discard them.

11. Return the pulled pork to the sauce. At this point the pork can be refrigerated for up to 1 week, frozen, or reheated and served immediately.

12. To serve in a sandwich: Place ½ to ¾ cup of the meat onto the bottom piece of a hamburger bun or onto a piece of sliced bread. Top the meat with about ¼ cup of coleslaw and cover with the top of the bun or another slice of bread. Serve immediately.

OVEN METHOD

1. Preheat the oven to 300°F.

2. Trim most of the external fat from the pork butt.

3. Heat the oil over medium to high heat in a heavy-gauge braising pot that is large enough to hold the meat comfortably and has a tight-fitting lid. Season the pork with 1 teaspoon of the black pepper and 1 teaspoon of the salt.

4. When the oil is near the smoke point (see Chef's Notes, page 36), add the pork to the pot and sear the meat on all sides. You want to achieve a caramelized, dark brown color while being careful not to burn the drippings in the pot.

5. While the pork is browning, combine the barbecue sauce, apple cider vinegar, brown sugar, red pepper flakes, and the remaining 1 teaspoon black pepper and 1 teaspoon salt in a small bowl.

6. When the pork has been seared on all sides, remove the pan from the heat. Remove the pork from the pot and reserve it, covered with aluminum foil. Pour out and discard all of the fat left in the pot. Deglaze the pot with the water, scraping the fond with a wooden spoon to loosen it from the pot. Taste the drippings. If they taste at all bitter, discard the burnt drippings and wash out the pot. When all the particles have been discarded, return the meat to the pot. If the drippings do not taste bitter, return the pork directly back to the pot with the loosened drippings. Sprinkle the pork with the cayenne.

7. Add the barbecue sauce mixture to the pot. Warm the sauce and pork over medium heat until the sauce just starts to bubble. Cover the pot with a tight-fitting lid and transfer to the oven.

BRAISING

8. Check the pot every 30 minutes to ensure that the mixture is gently simmering. If the sauce is boiling, reduce the heat; if the sauce isn't simmering at all, increase the heat by 25 degrees. Cook the pork, turning it over occasionally, until the meat slides easily off of a fork when punctured, about 12 hours for an 8-pound butt. The meat can also be checked with a thermometer; the pork is done when it has reached an internal temperature of 193°F.

9. When the pork has finished cooking, remove the pot from the oven and set aside. Allow the pork and the sauce to cool in the covered pot. Carefully skim as much fat as possible off of the sauce.

10. When cool enough to handle, remove the pork from the sauce and pull it into strips using two forks or your fingers. The meat can also be chopped into small ½- to ¾-inch chunks or strands using a knife. If you discover any large pieces of fat while pulling the meat, remove and discard them.

11. Return the pulled pork to the sauce. At this point the pork can be refrigerated for up to 1 week, frozen, or reheated immediately and served.

12. To serve as a sandwich, place ½ to ¾ cup of the meat onto the bottom piece of a hamburger bun or onto a piece of sliced bread. Top the meat with about ¼ cup of coleslaw and cover with the top of the bun or another slice of bread. Serve immediately.

You could replace the Classic Barbecue Sauce with your favorite barbecue sauce; a smoky sweet-and-sour sauce also works well.

Be sure to season the pork with the cayenne pepper only after searing it. Searing with the cayenne on the meat will create an unpleasant atmosphere in your kitchen that may cause burning eyes and coughing.

For a rough calculation you can figure a cooking time of 1½ hours per pound of meat. For example, an 8-pound pork butt will take about 12 hours to cook, using this recipe; if you use two 4-pound pork butts instead, then the cooking time will be half as long.

LOW AND SLOW

Traditional Braised Short Ribs

MAKES 4 SERVINGS

Beef short ribs are a highly flavorful cut of meat, and a low-and-slow cooking process, braising in this case, makes the meat so tender that you won't even need to use a knife (for this reason the term used for doneness is "fork-tender"). The rich, thick sauce is delicious served with Whipped Potatoes or Garlic Whipped Potatoes (page 173). When making this recipe, be sure to purchase at least 1 pound of ribs per portion, or 1 to 1½ pounds if you have hearty diners. Short ribs have a lot of bone and fat, and shrinkage during cooking will reduce the yield.

1. Preheat the oven to 300°F.

2. Trim the short ribs of any excess fat and gristle, and season with salt and black pepper.

3. Heat the oil in a large Dutch oven over high heat. Add the short ribs, and sear until browned on all sides, 10 to 15 minutes. This may require working in multiple batches or using more than one pot to avoid overcrowding. Do not overcrowd the pot, or the meat will steam and not brown. Remove the ribs from the pot and reserve. If you are searing in batches, deglaze the pan with some water after each batch and reserve the pan drippings. Clean the pot before browning the next batch.

4. Reduce the heat to medium. Add the carrot to the pot and cook, stirring occasionally, until just starting to brown on the edges, about 4 minutes. Add the onion and continue to cook, stirring occasionally, until the onion is a uniform golden brown, 7 to 8 minutes. Stir

4 lb beef short ribs, bone in

Kosher salt, as needed

Freshly ground black pepper, as needed

3 tbsp vegetable oil

1 carrot, diced

1 yellow onion, diced

2 tbsp tomato paste

1 cup dry red wine

3 tbsp all-purpose flour

2 cups beef broth, or as needed

1 bay leaf

¼ tsp dried thyme

Freshly cracked black pepper, as needed

in the tomato paste and cook until it darkens, about 1 minute. Deglaze the pot with the red wine, and continue to cook until no liquid remains. Add the flour and cook, stirring frequently, for 3 to 5 minutes to make a roux. Add the broth, whisking well to remove any lumps. Increase the heat to bring the mixture to a gentle simmer.

5. Return the ribs (and any reserved drippings) to the Dutch oven along with any juices that they released while resting. The liquid in the pot should reach halfway up the meat; if necessary, add more broth to adjust the level. Add the bay leaf and thyme. Cover the pot and transfer it to the oven.

6. After 20 minutes, check that the liquid is at a gentle simmer. If the liquid is boiling, reduce the oven temperature; if it is not simmering, increase the oven temperature. Every 20 minutes, turn the ribs to keep them evenly moistened and check that the cooking liquid is maintaining a gentle simmer. Continue cooking until the ribs are fork-tender, 1½ to 2 hours, depending on the size of the ribs. Transfer the ribs to a serving platter, moisten them with a little of the cooking liquid, and cover loosely with aluminum foil while completing the sauce. Remove and discard the bay leaf.

7. Skim as much fat as possible from the cooking liquid. Transfer the Dutch oven to the stovetop over high heat, and simmer until the cooking liquid is flavorful and has reached a pourable consistency, about 10 minutes. If necessary, adjust the seasoning with salt and cracked pepper. Strain the sauce, if desired.

8. Serve the ribs coated with the sauce.

BRAISING

Korean-Style Braised Short Ribs

The deep, rich flavor of the short ribs matches very well with the Asian flavor profile of the other ingredients. If desired, accompany them with steamed rice, snow peas, and kimchi. Nine pounds of ribs might seem to be too much, but after bone removal, trimming, the removal of excess fat, and shrinkage during cooking, you'll be left with just enough for 6 servings.

1. Preheat the oven to 400°F.

2. TO MAKE THE DRY RUB: Combine the salt, ground ginger, garlic powder, onion powder, pepper, and flour.

3. Toss the beef short ribs in the rub to thoroughly coat with as much of the rub as possible. Place the ribs, meat side up, onto a roasting rack and set the rack in a roasting pan. Roast for 30 minutes.

4. Add the onion, carrot, and garlic to the roasting pan underneath the rack and immediately return it to the oven. Continue roasting until the ribs look well browned, about 30 minutes. Remove the pan from the oven and reduce the oven temperature to 275°F.

5. Remove the ribs, vegetables, and rack from the roasting pan. Drain all of the fat from the bottom of the pan, and discard it. Return the ribs and vegetables directly to the pan.

6. In a bowl, combine the brown sugar, beef broth, mirin, vinegar, soy sauce, and fish sauce and stir to combine. Pour the mixture over the ribs.

DRY RUB

2 tbsp kosher salt

2 tbsp ground ginger

2 tbsp garlic powder

2 tbsp onion powder

2 tbsp freshly ground black pepper

¼ cup all-purpose flour

9 lb beef short ribs, bone in

1 cup diced onion

½ cup roughly chopped carrot

8 garlic cloves, peeled

½ cup packed dark brown sugar

2 cups beef broth

⅔ cup mirin (see Chef's Note)

½ cup rice wine vinegar

½ cup soy sauce

1 tbsp fish sauce

2 tbsp cornstarch

1 tbsp plus 2 tsp cold water

GARNISH

1 bunch green onions, sliced

7. Cover the pan tightly with aluminum foil. When the oven temperature has reached 275°F, return the pan to the oven. Adjust the oven temperature as necessary to keep the ribs at a very gentle simmer. After 2 hours, start checking the ribs for doneness by piercing them with a wooden skewer or a fork. When the skewer or fork pulls out without picking up any of the meat, the meat is tender and the ribs can be removed from the oven. The ribs may not all finish cooking at the same time; after checking for doneness, return any undercooked ribs to the oven to finish cooking. Keep the cooked ribs warm in a pan loosely covered with foil.

8. When all of the ribs have been removed from the pan, strain the cooking liquid from the bottom of the pan through a fine-mesh sieve into a 4-cup measuring container and reserve. Allow the container to sit at room temperature until the fat separates from the usable liquid and floats to the top.

9. Meanwhile, remove the meat from the bones and discard the bones. Trim the meat and remove any excess fat and connective tissues.

10. When the fat has completely separated from the reserved liquid, skim it off and discard it. You will need 2 cups of the liquid to prepare the sauce; if you don't have enough liquid after skimming the fat, add enough water to the liquid to make 2 cups. If you have more than 2 cups of liquid, transfer it to a small, uncovered sauce pot and cook over medium heat until the liquid has reduced to 2 cups.

11. In a separate container, combine the cornstarch and cold water to make a slurry, stirring until the mixture is smooth. In a small sauce pot over high heat, bring the 2 cups of liquid to a boil, then gradually pour in the slurry while whisking constantly. The sauce will immediately thicken. Quickly remove the pot from the heat and strain the sauce through a fine-mesh strainer.

12. Serve the ribs with the sauce and garnish with sliced green onions.

BRAISING

33

Beef Braised in Beer and Onions

At first glance, this may look like a huge quantity of onions, but it is not an error. Do not reduce the amount of onions in this recipe. They are what give the dish its outstanding deep, rich flavor, reminiscent of onion soup. The bitterness of the beer also balances out the sweetness of the onions. Oven-roasted root vegetables and most green vegetables go well with this dish, or it can be served with noodles, rice, or mashed potatoes.

1. Preheat the oven to 300°F.

2. Season the meat with salt and pepper. Heat the canola oil in a large Dutch oven over medium-high heat. When the oil in the pot just starts to smoke, add the meat and sear until nicely browned on all sides, about 5 minutes.

3. Remove the meat from the pot and set aside. Add the onions to the hot pot, reduce the heat to medium, and cook until they are a deep golden brown, about 30 minutes. (The browner the onions get, the more stirring you will have to do to make sure that they don't burn on the bottom of the pan.) Add the garlic and continue to cook until the garlic is soft, about 1 minute more.

4. Return the meat to the pot, and add the broth, beer, tomatoes, thyme, and bay leaf. Cover the pot and transfer it to the oven. Check the beef after 20 minutes and adjust the oven temperature as needed to keep the liquid at a very gentle simmer; if the liquid boils, the beef will be dry.

One 4-lb boneless chuck pot roast

1 tsp kosher salt, plus more as needed

½ tsp freshly cracked black pepper, plus more as needed

2 tbsp canola oil

4 medium onions, sliced (8 cups)

4 garlic cloves, minced

1 qt low-sodium beef broth

1 pt amber or red beer

One 14.5-oz can low-salt diced tomatoes

1 sprig thyme

1 bay leaf

LOW AND SLOW

5. Braise until the meat starts to become tender, about 1½ hours, turning the meat occasionally. Periodically check the stew to make sure it is not boiling and adjust the oven temperature as needed to maintain a very gentle simmer.

6. Uncover the pot and continue cooking until a fork inserted into the meat releases easily when it is pulled out, 30 minutes to 1 hour more.

7. Remove and discard the bay leaf. Cool the stew slightly at room temperature. To serve, slice the beef into ¼-inch-thick slices and serve immediately with the onions and sauce. Alternatively, you can refrigerate the stew overnight in an airtight container. (The flavor is often better if a braised item is allowed to chill so that some cooking liquid absorbs back into the meat. Chilling also makes it much easier to skim all the solid fat off the top before reheating.) Before slicing and serving, gently reheat the chilled stew slowly at a simmer (do not allow it to boil) until the meat reaches an internal temperature of 165°F.

CHEF'S NOTES

If heated to a high enough temperature, a fat will begin to break down, emit smoke, and develop an unpleasant flavor, which will ruin anything cooked in it. This temperature is known as the "smoke point." The smoke point is different for each type of fat; the smoke point for vegetable oils, including canola oil, is generally around 450°F.

Slow Cooker Method Place the seared meat, onion and garlic mixture, and beer, broth, tomatoes, thyme, and bay leaf in a slow cooker set on low heat. Cover and cook until the meat is fork-tender, about 6 hours.

If you would like to thicken the sauce, remove the beef, remove and discard the bay leaf, and whisk ½ teaspoon arrowroot or 1 tablespoon cornstarch into the cooking liquid while it is simmering. Alternatively, remove the beef and bay leaf and simmer the liquid over medium heat until reduced to the desired consistency. Return the beef to the sauce and serve.

New England Yankee Pot Roast

MAKES 6 SERVINGS

Although it is a traditional New England dish, there is no single "correct" way to make Yankee Pot Roast. True to Yankee practicality, the vegetables used in each family's recipe depended upon what produce was available and economical. Each family considers their recipe to be the best, and it remains a classic comfort food in New England today.

1. This dish can be cooked in the oven or on the stovetop. If using the oven, preheat the oven to 275°F.

2. Season the chuck roast with salt and pepper. Heat the oil in a large Dutch oven over high heat. When the oil in the pan just starts to smoke, add the chuck roast and sear it until browned on all sides, 10 to 15 minutes. Remove the beef from the pot and reserve.

3. Reduce the heat to medium. Add the diced carrot to the pot and cook, stirring occasionally, until just starting to brown on the edges, about 4 minutes. Add the diced onion and continue to cook, stirring occasionally, until the onion is a uniform golden brown, 7 to 8 minutes. Stir in the tomato paste and cook until it darkens, about 1 minute. Add the flour and cook, stirring frequently, for 2 to 3 minutes. Add the broth, whisking well to prevent any lumps. Increase the heat and bring the mixture to a gentle simmer.

4. Return the beef to the Dutch oven along with any juices that it released while resting. If the liquid level in the Dutch oven is not halfway up the meat, add water or more broth to adjust the level. Add the bay leaf and thyme.

One 4-lb boneless chuck roast

Kosher salt, as needed

Freshly ground black pepper, as needed

3 tbsp vegetable oil or canola oil

1 carrot, peeled and diced plus 3 carrots, peeled and cut into 1-inch pieces

1 yellow onion, diced

2 tbsp tomato paste

¼ cup all-purpose flour

4 cups beef broth, or as needed

1 bay leaf

½ tsp dried thyme or 6 sprigs thyme

12 to 18 pearl onions, fresh or frozen

(continued)

5. Adjust the heat under the Dutch oven until the liquid is just barely simmering, or place the Dutch oven in the oven. Using either method, the liquid should constantly be at a very gentle simmer and the meat should be turned occasionally during cooking. When the meat is fork-tender, after about 2½ hours, remove it from the Dutch oven. Cover the meat loosely with aluminum foil and reserve in a warm place.

2 parsnips, peeled and cut into 1-inch pieces (optional)

1 lb Red Bliss potatoes, peeled or unpeeled, cut into 1-inch pieces

1 cup peas, fresh or frozen

6. Strain the cooking liquid through a fine-mesh sieve and discard the solid contents. Skim off as much fat as possible. Return the liquid to the Dutch oven and bring to a boil over high heat. If the liquid is too thick, add enough water to achieve a consistency that will lightly coat the back of a wooden spoon. Add the pearl onions (if using fresh), parsnips, if using, potatoes, and the 1-inch carrot pieces to the liquid, cover the pot, and simmer until the vegetables begin to get tender, about 30 minutes. Add the peas and frozen onions (if not using fresh). Cover and simmer for 10 minutes more. At this point the liquid should have reduced into a light sauce.

7. Return the beef to the sauce to warm.

8. When warm, transfer the meat to a cutting board and carve it into 1-inch-thick slices against the grain. Transfer the carved meat to a warm serving platter or individual bowls and top with the vegetables and sauce.

Beef Chili

MAKES 6 SERVINGS

The question of whether beans "belong" in chili has been a matter of contention among chili cooks for a long time. Beans were added to chili to require less beef, stretch it out, and make it more economical. If you like beans in your chili, simply add a can of red kidney beans to this recipe.

1. Place the meat in the freezer for 3 hours. When it is partially frozen, cut the meat into ½-inch cubes or smaller. This will make the process easier, and the cuts will be more accurate.

2. If using whole spices, grind the cumin and coriander to a powder using a mortar and pestle. A spice grinder can also be used. In a bowl, combine the ground cumin and coriander with the sweet and medium chili powders, paprika, oregano, cinnamon, and cayenne.

3. In a food processor, purée the tomatoes, onion, garlic, chipotle peppers, jalapeño, tomato paste, and sugar until smooth. Reserve until needed.

4. Heat 1½ tablespoons of oil in each of 2 large heavy-bottomed or cast-iron pans. If you only have one pan, you will need to work in small batches, deglazing the pan with some water in between batches; do not overload the pans with meat or it will boil and turn gray.

5. Add the meat to the pans and cook until browned on all sides, about 10 minutes. When the meat is brown, transfer it to a 2- or 3-quart pot over medium heat.

3 lb boneless beef shoulder

1 tbsp whole cumin seeds, or 2 tsp ground cumin

1 tbsp whole coriander seeds, or 2 tsp ground coriander

1 tbsp sweet chili powder

1 tbsp medium hot chili powder

1 tbsp smoked Spanish paprika

1 tsp dried oregano

½ tsp ground cinnamon

¼ tsp cayenne pepper

One 14.5-oz can whole plum tomatoes

2 cups chopped onion

8 garlic cloves, roughly chopped

3 canned chipotles in adobo sauce, chopped

6. Add the ground spice mixture to the pot to quickly toast the spices in the remaining fat with the meat.

7. Deglaze the pan with the beer. Stir to pick up any caramelized bits on the bottom of the pan, add the puréed tomato mixture to the pot, and bring to a boil over high heat. Reduce the heat to establish a gentle simmer, then add the salt. Continue simmering until the meat is tender, 2 to 2½ hours. If the chili reduces down and becomes too thick during cooking, add some water to adjust the consistency; if there is not enough moisture, the meat will not cook properly.

8. When the meat is tender, add the lime juice.

9. Serve the chili in bowls. Top each portion with 1 tablespoon each of cheese and sour cream and garnish with cilantro leaves.

1 jalapeño, seeds and veins removed, roughly chopped

2 tbsp tomato paste

1 tsp sugar

3 tbsp vegetable, corn, or canola oil

12 oz beer

1½ tsp kosher salt

1 tbsp fresh lime juice

GARNISH

¼ cup plus 2 tbsp shredded cheddar cheese

¼ cup plus 2 tbsp sour cream

Cilantro leaves, as needed

CHEF'S NOTES

Slow Cooker Method Instead of combining the ingredients in a 2- or 3-quart pot, combine them in the slow cooker. Add the beer and salt, and cook with the chili barely at a simmer.

This is a spicy chili. If you want to tone down the heat, remove the cayenne and/or omit one of the chipotle peppers.

Osso Buco

Osso buco is a classic dish that utilizes the tough shanks of veal. Despite the shanks being a well-exercised, bony cut, the braising process produces a tender and succulent meat with a very deep-flavored sauce. When this dish is served, the rich bone marrow should also be scooped out with a spoon and consumed. There is a high bone-to-meat ratio, so it will take about 1 pound of veal shanks to produce one portion of osso buco.

1. Preheat the oven to 300°F.

2. Heat the oil in a Dutch oven over high heat until it starts to shimmer. Meanwhile, season the veal shanks with salt and pepper and dust with the flour. Put the shanks into the Dutch oven, and sear on all sides in the hot oil until browned, about 10 minutes. It is important not to overcrowd the pot, so this may require working in multiple batches or using more than one pot. Do not overcrowd the pots or the meat will steam and not brown. Remove the meat from the pot and reserve.

3. Add the carrot to the Dutch oven with the remaining fat. Sauté over medium-high heat until the edges of the carrots just start to brown, about 5 minutes. Add the onion and sauté until caramelized, about 5 minutes more.

4. Deglaze the pot with one-third of the wine and continue cooking until all the wine has evaporated and only the fat and vegetables remain. Add the garlic and tomato paste and cook, stirring constantly, until the tomato paste turns brown, about 1 minute.

¼ cup olive oil

6 lb veal shanks, crosscut, 1½ inches thick

1½ tsp kosher salt, plus more as needed

1 tsp freshly cracked black pepper, plus more as needed

½ cup all-purpose flour

¼ cup small-dice carrot

½ cup small-dice onion

½ cup dry white wine

1 tsp minced garlic

2 tbsp tomato paste

4 cups beef broth, or as needed

1 bay leaf

3 sprigs thyme

GREMOLATA

1 tbsp minced garlic

2 tbsp grated lemon zest

2 tbsp chopped flat-leaf parsley

1 tsp minced anchovy

5. Add another one-third of the wine and reduce until all the wine has evaporated. Add the remaining one-third of the wine, and cook until the pot is dry. Turn off the heat.

6. Return the veal shanks to the Dutch oven and add enough broth to cover by two-thirds. Add the bay leaf and thyme and bring to a simmer over medium-high heat. Immediately transfer to the oven. Adjust the oven temperature as needed to maintain a very gentle simmer throughout the cooking time.

7. Braise until the meat is fork-tender, 2 to 2½ hours. Test this by inserting a two-prong fork or a skewer into the center of the meat. If the meat slides easily from the fork or skewer it is done. Remove the veal from the liquid and reserve, covered, in a warm place. Remove and discard the bay leaf.

8. Return the Dutch oven with the cooking liquid to the stovetop over medium heat and reduce until the sauce is thick enough to coat the back of a spoon and has attained a good flavor. If necessary, season with additional salt and pepper.

9. **TO MAKE THE GREMOLATA:** Combine the garlic, lemon zest, parsley, and anchovy.

10. To serve, pour the sauce over the veal and sprinkle the gremolata on top. Serve immediately.

Slow Cooker Method Follow the method through step 4. Do not return the meat to the Dutch oven. Instead, combine the veal, vegetable, and tomato mixture with the broth, bay leaf, and thyme inside the slow cooker. Cook for 8 hours on the low setting or for 6 hours on high.

Serve the osso buco with Saffron Rice Pilaf (see Chef's Note, page 202) or, if you're feeling adventurous, with saffron risotto.

BRAISING

Braised Oxtails

MAKES 6 SERVINGS

Oxtails are not from an ox, they are from cattle. Don't be squeamish about them. They are delicious, intensely flavorful meat. There is a high bone-to-meat ratio, so you will need at least 1 pound per person. The high bone ratio also adds more flavor and viscosity to the sauce. This dish pairs well with Whipped Potatoes or Garlic Whipped Potatoes (page 173).

1. Preheat the oven to 300°F.

2. Heat the oil in a Dutch oven or ovenproof pot with a tight-fitting lid until it starts to shimmer. Meanwhile, season the oxtails with the salt and pepper.

3. Add the oxtails to the pot and sear on all sides until well caramelized, about 10 minutes. This may require working in multiple batches or using more than one pot. Do not overcrowd the pots or the meat will steam and not brown.

4. Remove and reserve the oxtails and deglaze the pot with the water. When the water evaporates, add the small-dice carrot to the fat remaining in the pot. Cook, stirring, until the edges start to turn brown.

5. Add the onion and continue to cook until the carrots and onions are browned and caramelized. Add the tomato paste and cook, stirring, until it loses its red color. Deglaze the pot with ½ cup of the wine. Stir and reduce until the wine has evaporated and the tomato paste starts to brown. Add the remaining ½ cup wine and continue to cook until the wine has evaporated.

¼ cup vegetable oil

6 lb oxtails, cut into 2-inch-thick sections, trimmed of external fat

1 tbsp kosher salt, plus more as needed

1 tsp freshly ground black pepper, plus more as needed

¼ cup water

½ cup small-dice carrot, plus 1 cup large-dice carrot

1 cup small-dice onion

2 tbsp tomato paste

1 cup dry red wine

6. Add the flour to the pot and stir for 1 to 2 minutes.

7. Add the beef stock, garlic, thyme, and bay leaf, whisking to prevent lumps. Add the reserved oxtails. The liquid in the pot should reach halfway up the meat; if necessary, add more broth or water to adjust the level. Bring the stock to a simmer.

8. Cover the pot and transfer it to the oven. Braise the oxtails for about 2 hours, turning them at the 1 hour point.

9. Add the large-dice carrot, turnips, rutabaga, and celeriac and braise for another 30 minutes, or until the meat is fork-tender and the vegetables are fully cooked.

10. Remove the vegetables and meat from the pot, cover lightly, and reserve in a warm place. Remove and discard the bay leaf.

11. Return the pot to the stovetop and bring the liquid to a simmer. Cook, skimming away excess fat, until it has thickened and developed a good flavor. Season with additional salt and pepper if needed and then strain into a bowl.

12. Serve the oxtails with the sauce and vegetables.

1 rounded tbsp all-purpose flour

3 cups beef stock or broth, or as needed

1 garlic clove, chopped

6 sprigs thyme or ½ tsp dried thyme

1 bay leaf

1 cup large-dice white turnips

1 cup large-dice rutabaga

1 cup large-dice celeriac (celery root), or peeled celery, cut into 1-inch pieces

CHEF'S NOTE

Slow Cooker Method At step 8 when all of the braising ingredients are combined, they can be transferred to a slow cooker. They will take up to 8 hours to cook on the low setting. Add the vegetables 1½ to 2 hours before the meat is fork-tender. Proceed with the remaining steps.

Braised Lamb Shanks

This dish is fall and winter comfort food. The shanks are packed with flavor and the long, slow cooking process makes them tender, juicy, and succulent while yielding a rich sauce.

1. Preheat the oven to 300°F.

2. Season the lamb shanks with salt and pepper.

3. Heat the oil in a 9 by 13-inch braiser or Dutch oven (or any pot that can accommodate the shanks and be covered with a lid or aluminum foil) over high heat. Add the shanks, and sear them until browned on all sides, about 10 minutes. Remove the shanks from the pot and reserve. This may require working in multiple batches or using more than one pot to avoid overcrowding. Do not overcrowd the pot or the meat will steam and not brown.

4. Pour off all but 2 tablespoons of the cooking fat from the pot. Add the parsnips or carrot and cook over medium to high heat until they start to caramelize, about 10 minutes. Add the onion and continue to cook until the onion is golden brown in color, about 2 minutes more. Add one-third of the wine, and continue cooking to reduce the wine until only the fat is remaining in the pot. Add the tomato paste and cook, stirring constantly, for 2 minutes to reduce. Stir in another one-third of the wine to thin out the tomato paste, and continue cooking until the wine has evaporated. Add the final one-third of the wine and continue cooking until all of the wine has evaporated.

6 to 8 lb lamb shanks

Kosher salt, as needed

Freshly cracked black pepper, as needed

3 tbsp vegetable oil

1 cup peeled, medium-dice parsnips or carrot

1 cup medium-dice onion

2 cups red wine

3 tbsp tomato paste

¼ cup all-purpose flour

1 qt beef or lamb broth

1 bay leaf

CHEF'S NOTES

Slow Cooker Method At the point in step 5 where the broth and meat are combined, add everything to your slow cooker and proceed as suggested by the manufacturer.

This dish goes well with Spoonbread (page 205).

5. Reduce the heat to low, add the flour, and stir until the flour turns reddish brown, about 4 minutes. Whisk in the broth and add the bay leaf and lamb shanks. Increase the heat to establish a simmer.

6. Cover the pot and transfer it to the oven. Periodically check the shanks to make sure that the cooking liquid is simmering, making adjustments to the oven temperature as necessary to maintain a simmer. Continue cooking until the shanks are fork-tender, about 1½ hours. To check for tenderness, pierce the shanks with a fork or bamboo skewer, and when the meat does not hang on the fork or skewer they are tender enough be removed from the cooking liquid. Remove the shanks from the pot and reserve.

7. Return the pot of cooking liquid to the stovetop over medium heat and simmer, skimming off as much fat as possible, until the sauce has reached a consistency that will coat the back of a wooden spoon. Strain the sauce and serve with the lamb shanks.

BRAISING

Pork Braised in Milk

This variation of the classic Italian dish was inspired by Marcella Hazan, a world-renowned writer on Italian cuisine. This dish does not have a traditional silky smooth meat sauce because the caramelized milk curds that form during the braising process become the sauce. It's a unique dish in both preparation and flavor.

1. Season the pork with salt and pepper.

2. Heat the oil and butter in a Dutch oven over medium-high heat. Add the pork and cook until browned on all sides, about 2 minutes per side. Reduce the heat to medium. Slowly pour the warm milk into the pot with the pork and increase the heat. Bring the liquid to a boil, then immediately reduce the heat to low.

3. Tightly cover the pot and cook gently over low heat, turning occasionally, until the pork is tender and reaches an internal temperature of 190°F, about 4 hours. If the liquid level gets too low during the cooking process, add more warm milk. Remove the pork from the pot. Loosely cover with aluminum foil, and set it aside to rest.

4. Remove as much fat as possible from the pot. If the milk has already browned lightly and started to form curds, use a wooden spoon to scrape the bottom of the pot to loosen the curds. If curds have not yet formed, place the pot over medium-high heat and cook until the milk begins to reduce. Once the curds have formed, use a wooden spoon to scrape

One 2½- to 3-lb pork butt or shoulder, bone in

Kosher salt, as needed

Freshly ground black pepper, as needed

2 tbsp olive oil

2 tbsp butter

5 cups whole milk, warm, plus more as needed

the bottom of the pot to loosen the curds. Continue cooking over medium-high heat until the milk has almost completely reduced but the curds remain and are slightly browned. The finished sauce is supposed to look like moist, lumpy curds that resemble scrambled eggs, rather than a traditional, smooth sauce. If there is any excess fat remaining in the pot, pour it out and discard it.

5. Cut the pork into 1-inch-thick pieces and serve with the sauce.

Slow Cooker Method Sear the meat in a pot as described in step 2. Remove it from the pot and place it into the slow cooker. Add one-third of the milk to the searing pot, to dissolve the pork bits and pieces on the bottom of the pot, then transfer it to the slow cooker. Add the remaining milk to the slow cooker. Set the slow cooker to low, cover, and cook, turning the pork over occasionally, until the pork is tender and reaches an internal temperature of 190°F, about 8 hours. Remove the pork and cut into 1-inch-thick pieces. Since the milk will not caramelize in the slow cooker, transfer the milk sauce to a pan over medium heat and reduce until the milk has caramelized as described at left. Serve the sauce with the pork.

BRAISING

Ragú Bolognese

Bolognese is essentially a meat stew with a small amount of tomato added—although Americans often confuse it for a tomato sauce with some meat added. The sauce is cooked slowly to develop a deep, rich flavor. In Italy it is traditionally served with tagliatelle pasta and Parmigiano-Reggiano, but you may choose another pasta if you'd like. It is also delicious in lasagna.

1. In a Dutch oven or saucepan, warm the butter over medium heat. Add the onion, celery, carrot, and garlic. Cover and cook until the onions are transparent, about 10 minutes.

2. Meanwhile, heat the olive oil in a 10- to 12-inch heavy-bottomed or cast-iron pan over medium heat, and bring it just to the smoke point (see Chef's Notes, page 36), the point at which you start to see small wisps of smoke coming from the hot oil. Working in small batches, add some of the pancetta, veal, pork, and beef to the pan. Add enough meat to cover three-quarters of the surface area of the pan. Increase the heat to high. You should only add an amount of meat that can brown lightly without burning or boiling in its own juices as they render; you will need to do this in several batches in order to avoid overcrowding the pan. Cook each batch of meat until the fat renders and the meat is browned, 10 to 16 minutes. Transfer the meat to the Dutch oven, or to a slow cooker along with the vegetable mixture.

4 tbsp butter

1 cup diced onion

1 cup peeled, small-dice celery

1 cup peeled, small-dice carrot

6 garlic cloves, peeled and chopped

2 tbsp olive oil

¼ lb pancetta, finely chopped

1 lb ground veal

1 lb ground pork

½ lb 85 percent ground beef

¾ cup whole milk

One 14.5-oz can whole plum tomatoes

2 cups beef broth, plus more as needed

3. When all the meat has been browned, add the milk to the Dutch oven or slow cooker. Simmer over high heat until all of the milk has reduced and there is none left in the pot. Add the tomatoes, crushing them with your hand before adding them to the pot. Simmer for about 15 minutes more. Add the beef broth and wine, increase the heat to bring the mixture to a boil, then reduce the heat to establish a gentle simmer. Simmer, uncovered, for 2 hours in the Dutch oven, or 3 to 4 hours on low in the slow cooker, adding more broth if necessary during cooking. At the end of the cooking time, the consistency should be thick and heavy.

1 cup white wine

1½ lb fresh tagliatelle pasta (page 184), or dried pasta

⅓ cup kosher salt, plus more as needed

Freshly ground black pepper, as needed

4 oz freshly grated Parmigiano-Reggiano

4. Ten minutes before serving, add the pasta to a large pot with 6 quarts of boiling salted water and season with ⅓ cup of salt. Boil the pasta, stirring occasionally, until al dente, 8 to 10 minutes for fresh pasta, or according to the package instructions. (The Italian term *al dente* means "to the tooth" or "to the bite," referring to the need to chew the pasta due to its firmness.) Drain the pasta.

5. To serve, season the sauce with salt and pepper as needed. Pour the ragú over the cooked pasta and top with the cheese.

Chicken Curry

Chicken breasts would generally be used in a curry, so you can easily substitute strips of boneless, skinless chicken breast in this recipe if you prefer. However, the bone-in thighs have more flavor than breasts. They also have more moisture, so there is less of a tendency to dry out during cooking. Serve the chicken with white or basmati Rice Pilaf (page 202), broccoli or cauliflower, and naan bread.

1. Combine the ginger, garlic, and yogurt in a 1-gallon zip-close plastic bag. Stir or squeeze to combine the ingredients well. Add the chicken, remove as much air as possible from the bag, seal, and place in the refrigerator overnight.

2. Combine the crushed chiles and onion in a food processor. Purée until smooth.

3. Heat the oil in a large pot over low heat. Add the coriander, garam masala, turmeric, and black pepper and lightly toast the spices, about 1 minute.

4. Add the chile-onion mixture, coconut, and cinnamon. Increase the heat to bring the mixture to a boil, then reduce the heat and simmer for 10 minutes. Remove the pot from the heat, and add the coconut milk, chicken with its marinade, and the ground almonds.

1½ tbsp finely grated ginger

1 tbsp minced garlic

¾ cup plain yogurt

2½ lb skinless chicken thighs, bone in (2 thighs per person)

2 dried red chiles, crushed

2 cups finely chopped yellow onion

1 tbsp vegetable oil

1 tbsp ground coriander

1 tsp garam masala

1 tsp ground turmeric

¼ tsp freshly cracked black pepper

5. Bring the mixture to a very gentle simmer over medium heat. Simmer until the chicken is tender, 30 to 40 minutes. Stir in the lemon juice and adjust the seasoning with salt as needed.

6. Transfer to a serving bowl and top with the cilantro.

CHEF'S NOTES

Slow Cooker Method Transfer the chicken mixture from the pan to the slow cooker after completing step 4. Cook on the low setting until the chicken is tender, about 2 hours. Stir in the lemon juice and adjust the seasoning with salt if necessary. Serve as described above.

For a very smooth sauce, remove the cooked chicken from the sauce and place it in the serving bowl, then, using a blender or immersion blender, blend the sauce until smooth before adding it to the serving bowl.

Make sure that you use coconut milk and not coconut water or coconut cream. Coconut milk is unsweetened and has a rich and creamy consistency.

2 tbsp sweetened flaked coconut

1 tsp ground cinnamon

¾ cup unsweetened coconut milk

2 tbsp ground almonds

1 tsp fresh lemon juice

Kosher salt, as needed

2 tbsp chopped cilantro

Moroccan Chicken Tagine with Tomato, Chickpeas, and Apricots

A tagine is a dish originating in North Africa that is named for the earthenware pot in which the stew is cooked. The ingredients are placed in a shallow, round clay dish and covered with a conical cover that has a knob on top. The cover is designed to trap moisture within the tagine during cooking so that the contents slowly braise inside, making the meat incredibly tender. In this recipe, a slow cooker takes the place of the traditional tagine. Because chicken is a tender cut of meat, take great care not to overcook it, which will dry it out. If desired, serve this dish with couscous or Rice Pilaf (page 202).

1. Preheat the oven to 300°F.

2. Heat the oil in a sauté pan over medium heat. Add the onions and garlic, and sweat them until they become soft and translucent, about 4 minutes. Add the coriander, cinnamon, cumin, and cayenne, if using. Warm the spices, stirring constantly, for about 1 minute. Deglaze the pan with a little of the chicken broth. Transfer the mixture to a slow cooker.

3. Place the 8 chicken pieces into the slow cooker on top of the onion mixture. Cover with the canned tomatoes with their juices, the remaining chicken broth, and the chickpeas, apricots, ginger, honey, and saffron or turmeric.

4. Cover and cook until the largest piece of chicken reaches an internal temperature of 165° to 170°F, about 6 hours with the slow cooker set on low or about 4 hours with the slow cooker set on high.

2 tbsp extra-virgin olive oil

2 yellow onions, diced into ¼-inch pieces

4 garlic cloves, finely chopped

1 tsp ground coriander

1 tsp ground cinnamon

1 tsp ground cumin

½ tsp cayenne pepper (optional; see Chef's Notes)

1 cup chicken broth

One 3- to 4-lb chicken, cut into 8 pieces (see Chef's Notes)

One 28-oz can chopped tomatoes

½ lb cooked dried chickpeas or two 14.5-oz cans chickpeas (see Chef's Notes)

5. While the chicken is cooking, toast the slivered almonds in the oven until they are a light golden brown, about 10 minutes.

6. When the chicken reaches the appropriate temperature, adjust the seasoning with salt and pepper if needed. Transfer the chicken to a serving platter or individual plates and top with the toasted almonds, cilantro leaves, and a squeeze of fresh lemon juice.

CHEF'S NOTES

For a mild spiciness, add the ½ teaspoon cayenne. If you prefer more heat, add 1 teaspoon cayenne.

The chicken should be divided into 8 pieces: 2 breasts split into halves, 2 drumsticks, and 2 thighs. Remove the backbone and wing tips and reserve them for another use. You can also purchase whole cut chickens at most grocery stores.

Dried chickpeas will provide a better flavor and texture in this dish. If you are using dried chickpeas, they will need to be soaked and cooked according to the package instructions. If using canned chickpeas, drain the chickpeas and rinse under cold water before using.

1 cup dried apricots, halved

One 1-inch piece ginger, grated or very finely chopped

3 tbsp honey

Pinch of saffron or 1 tsp ground turmeric

⅓ cup slivered almonds

Kosher salt, as needed

Freshly ground black pepper, as needed

½ cup lightly packed cilantro leaves

1 lemon, cut into wedges

Chicken Poêlé

MAKES 4 SERVINGS

Poêlé, or "butter roasting," is the French term for the process of cooking an item, such as chicken, slowly in its own fat and juices. This dish requires a lot of butter for flavoring and for basting during the cooking process, then all the fats, juices, and aromatic vegetables are served along with the meat. If desired, accompany this dish with rice or boiled barley.

1. Preheat the oven to 300°F.

2. Rinse the chicken in cool water. Remove the sack of neck, liver, and giblets from inside the chicken cavity; reserve the neck and discard the rest. Cut any excess fat away from the chicken.

3. Liberally season the chicken inside and out with salt and pepper. Arrange the butter on top of the chicken's breasts and legs. Fill the cavity with the rosemary and 4 sprigs of the thyme. Set aside.

4. Place the ham, onion, carrot, celery, and mushrooms in the bottom of a Dutch oven. Add the wine, bay leaves, the remaining 4 sprigs thyme, and the chicken neck. Place the chicken into the pot on top of the vegetable mixture.

5. Cover the pot and transfer it to the oven. Every 20 minutes during the first hour of cooking, baste the chicken with the juices that collect in the bottom of the pot. After 1 hour, increase the oven temperature to 350°F and uncover the pot to allow the chicken to brown as

One 4-lb whole chicken

Kosher salt, as needed

Freshly cracked white or black pepper, as needed

4 tbsp butter, cut into ⅛-inch-thick slices

2 sprigs rosemary

8 sprigs thyme

3 oz smoked ham, cut into ⅛-inch-thick slices

½ cup peeled, sliced white onion, cut ⅛ inch thick

½ cup sliced carrot, cut ⅛ inch thick

½ cup peeled, sliced celery, cut ⅛ inch thick

½ cup button mushrooms, stems removed, cut into ⅛-inch-thick slices

1 cup white wine

2 bay leaves

Finely chopped flat-leaf parsley, as needed (optional)

BRAISING

57

it finishes cooking. (Do not baste once it is cooking uncovered.) When the chicken has reached an internal temperature of 165°F in the thigh area, remove the pot from the oven, and allow the chicken to rest in the pot for 20 minutes before carving.

6. Remove the chicken, bay leaves, thyme, and chicken neck from the pot. The mixture of wine, chicken juices, butter, ham, and chicken fat that collects in the bottom of the pan provides the sauce and vegetable garnish for this dish. Taste the sauce, and adjust the seasoning with salt and pepper as needed.

7. To serve, place the sauce in a casserole dish or a serving bowl on the side. Carve the chicken and arrange it in the casserole dish. Garnish with parsley, if desired.

CHEF'S NOTE

Classically this sauce is served straight from the pan, and it tastes most delicious that way. In today's fat-conscious society, you may be tempted to skim off some of the fat, but I strongly caution you not to remove it all, because that's where the sauce's flavor is.

East Coast Bouillabaisse

This recipe is a spin-off of the classic French seafood stew. The fish is cooked slowly in the broth; using a slow cooker will work, but using the stovetop will give you more control over the fish as it cooks.

1. **To make the aioli:** Combine the mayonnaise, garlic, hot pepper sauce, and lemon juice. Taste the aioli, and adjust the seasoning with salt, pepper, hot sauce, and lemon juice, as needed. Chill until ready to use.

2. **To prepare the lobster:** Cut the lobster into 8 usable pieces: 2 claws, 2 arms, and 4 tail pieces. Working with the remaining body, pull the shell off of the top. Rinse the shell under cold water to remove anything that may discolor the broth and reserve. Chop the body into 4 to 6 pieces.

3. **To make the broth:** Heat the oil in a Dutch oven or large pot over low heat. Add the garlic and shallot and cook, covered, until translucent, about 10 minutes. Add the leeks, onion, fennel, lobster shell, and chopped lobster body, cover the pan, and sweat until the onions are wilted and translucent, about 15 minutes. Stir in the tomato paste. Add the fish broth or clam juice, white wine, and tomatoes. Increase the heat to establish a gentle simmer. Simmer, uncovered, until the leeks and onions are tender, about 20 minutes. Stir in the orange juice, bay leaf, thyme, and saffron.

AIOLI

2 tbsp mayonnaise

½ tsp minced garlic

2 drops hot pepper sauce, plus more as needed

Fresh lemon juice, as needed

Kosher salt, as needed

Freshly ground black pepper, as needed

One 2-lb lobster

BROTH

2 tbsp olive oil

2 tbsp minced garlic

1 tbsp minced shallot

1½ cups sliced leeks, white portion only, cut into ½-inch slices on the diagonal

1½ cups sliced onion, cut into ⅛-inch-thick slices with the grain

1½ cups sliced fennel, cut ⅛ inch thick (reserve the fronds)

BRAISING

(continued)

59

4. When the leeks and onion are tender, remove the lobster shell and body. Then add the bass, shrimp, mussels, and lobster claw, arm, and tail pieces to the broth. This will drop the temperature substantially, so turn up the heat to keep the broth's temperature in the 165° to 185°F range. Continue to simmer until all of the seafood is cooked, about 10 minutes (see Chef's Note). Season with salt and pepper as needed. Remove and discard the bay leaf. Add the parsley and fennel leaves.

5. Just before serving, toast the baguette slices in a toaster or toaster oven, and spread each with 1 teaspoon of the aioli.

6. To serve, divide the seafood among 6 warm bowls, then divide the vegetables and broth among the bowls. Top each bowl with two aioli croutons. Alternatively, this stew can be served family-style in a soup tureen with a ladle.

CHEF'S NOTE

The combination of seafood described in this recipe should finish cooking at about the same time. However, depending on the combination of seafood you use, you may need to add each seafood item in order of cooking time, rather than all at once. In the event that any of the seafood looks like it's starting to overcook, remove it from the broth, wait for the remaining fish to cook, then add it back to the stew at the end.

2 tbsp tomato paste

1 qt fish broth or clam juice

¾ cup white wine

1½ cups chopped canned or fresh tomatoes, peeled and seeded

Juice of 1 orange

1 bay leaf

6 sprigs thyme

¼ tsp saffron, or as needed

1¼ lb sea bass (or any white lean fish)

18 shrimp, shell on (21/25 count)

30 mussels or littleneck clams

Kosher salt, as needed

Freshly ground black pepper, as needed

2 tbsp chopped flat-leaf parsley

2 tbsp chopped fennel leaves (reserved from the fennel used for the broth)

12 slices baguette, cut ½ inch thick on the diagonal

Pappardelle with Duck Ragout

MAKES 4 SERVINGS

This is a classic Italian dish that uses inexpensive duck legs to make the braised ragout. Pappardelle is a wide, flat pasta that is good for serving with heartier, thicker sauces like this one. You can prepare fresh pappardelle or simply use packaged pasta.

1. If needed, cut the mushrooms into bite-size pieces. Place them in a small bowl and cover with the chicken broth. Set aside and allow to rehydrate until they are soft, at least 30 minutes.

2. Heat the olive oil in a Dutch oven over medium-high heat. Season the duck legs with salt and pepper, and add to the pot. Sear the legs on all sides until deep brown, about 4 minutes per side. This may require working in multiple batches or using more than one pot to avoid overcrowding. Do not overcrowd the pot or the meat will steam and not brown. Remove the duck legs from the pot and reduce the heat to medium.

3. Add the onions, shallots, and garlic to the pot. Cover and cook until the onions are soft and transparent, about 8 minutes. Remove the cover, and add the carrots, celery, red pepper flakes, and tomato paste. Stir to combine and cook until slightly browned, about 2 minutes.

4. Add ½ cup of the red wine and continue cooking until all of the wine has evaporated and the tomato paste has started to brown again, about 5 minutes. Add the remaining 1 cup wine and deglaze the pan. Add the

1 cup dried porcini mushrooms

1 cup chicken broth, warm

2 tbsp olive oil

3 lb duck legs, bone in, thighs and drumsticks attached, all skin and excess fat removed

Kosher salt, as needed

Freshly cracked black pepper, as needed

2 medium yellow onions, diced

2 shallots, minced

2 garlic cloves, minced

2 medium carrots, diced

1 rib celery, diced

½ tsp crushed red pepper flakes

tomatoes and their juices, the mushrooms, and all but 1 tablespoon of the chicken broth (see Chef's Notes). Add the thyme and duck legs and increase the heat to bring the mixture to a boil.

5. Cover the pot, reduce the heat to low to establish a very gentle simmer, and simmer until the duck is tender, about 2 hours.

6. When the duck is tender, remove it from the pot and set aside until it is cool enough to handle. Pull the meat from the bones and cut it into bite-size pieces. Discard the bones, and return the meat to the ragout. If necessary, adjust the seasoning with additional salt and black pepper.

7. To serve, top the cooked pasta with the duck ragout.

2 tbsp tomato paste

1½ cups dry red wine, preferably Chianti

One 28-oz can plum tomatoes with juice, preferably San Marzano, chopped

6 to 8 sprigs thyme (or ½ tsp dried thyme)

8 oz dried pappardelle pasta or 12 oz fresh pappardelle pasta (see page 184), cooked and drained (see Chef's Notes)

CHEF'S NOTES

Whenever a recipe includes the liquid used to soak dried mushrooms, pour all but 1 tablespoon of the soaking liquid into the preparation; that way any sand or debris stays in the bottom of the container and can be easily discarded.

Pappardelle is a very wide noodle. If working with fresh pasta dough (page 184), roll out the pasta dough to ¹⁄₁₆ inch thick. Using a sharp knife, cut 6-inch-long strips that are ¾ to 1 inch wide. To cook, boil in at least 1 gallon of boiling water and about 2 tablespoons of salt for every pound of fresh pasta. The cooked pasta should be tender and feel velvety smooth on the palate, not al dente. Drain before serving.

3 BARBECUING

THE SOURCE OF THE WORD *BARBECUE* IS DEBATABLE, BUT THE MOST POPULAR THEORY IS THAT IT CAME FROM THE WEST INDIES WHERE NATIVES WERE OBSERVED COOKING MEAT OVER AN OPEN FIRE ON GREENWOOD STICKS. IN SPANISH THE LATTICE OF GREENWOOD BRANCHES WERE CALLED *BARBACOA*, WHICH EVENTUALLY BECAME THE WORD "BARBECUE." ALTHOUGH WE COMMONLY USE IT, INCORRECTLY, TO REFER TO BOTH GRILLING AND THE GRILL ITSELF, THE PROPER DEFINITION IS THE LOW-AND-SLOW COOKING PROCESS DESCRIBED IN THIS CHAPTER: COOKING MEAT USING DRY HEAT, AT A LOW TEMPERATURE, WITH THE APPLICATION OF SMOKE FOR FLAVOR.

THE TECHNIQUE IS RESERVED for less tender meats with a higher fat content and the heat source for barbecue is all or partially fueled by wood or other products that will provide smoke. The product is cooked low and slow, gently infusing it with the flavor of smoke while the tenderizing process is going on. This technique is becoming increasingly popular with restaurant chefs and home cooks alike. Hundreds of barbecue competitions and rib fests around the country attract thousands of people and offer inspiration for practicing the art of barbecue at home. It is easy to get started with equipment you already have or by making a small investment.

All countries have their own unique style of barbecue, and in the United States, every region does too. The colonists in the New World started barbecuing meats in the 1600s, and curing, smoking, and drying meats to preserve them. As settlers moved across the country, they ate the resources that were most abundant in each region. In the South, that meant swine; in Kentucky, it was lamb or mutton, as a by-product of the wool trade—they would throw their aging animals over open pits to cook. In Texas and the Western states, beef became the meat of choice. They, too, would roast their older animals over an open pit, and this process was the start of regional barbecue.

But regional barbecue isn't only defined by the type of meat; it's more complicated than that. The smoky flavors of the most commonly available woods, a preference for "dry" or "wet" barbecue, and the flavor profiles of the seasonings all contribute to distinct regional styles. Mesquite is used in Texas, for example, and hickory in Kansas City. People in Memphis prefer their ribs dry—coated only with a dry spice mix—while in St. Louis ribs are slathered with sauce. Sauces vary widely from thick or thin, tomato-, mustard-, or vinegar-based, sweet or spicy.

REGIONAL BARBECUE

REGION	MEAT	SAUCE	WOOD	FLAVOR PROFILE
North Carolina, East	Whole hog	Thin, vinegar-based, no tomato	Hickory, sometimes oak	Spicy, black pepper, red pepper flakes, cayenne pepper
North Carolina, West	Pork shoulder, butts	Thin, vinegar-based with ketchup and molasses or sugar	Hickory, sometimes oak	Spicy, sweet, tomato
South Carolina	Pork butt, ribs	Thin, mustard- and vinegar-based, some areas tomato-based	Hickory, oak	Varies depending on region from sweet and acidic to fiery
Memphis, Tennessee	Pork, ribs, St. Louis–style cut ribs, and shoulder	Ribs are dry, sauce served on the side	Hickory	Thin, tangy, sweet
Kansas City, Missouri	Pork, beef, chicken	Thick, tomato- and vinegar-based with spices	Hickory, oak	Sweet, sour, sometimes spicy
Kentucky	Mutton (1+ year lamb)	Thick, tomato-based, black, with Worcestershire sauce, bourbon	Hickory	Sweet, sour, spicy
Texas, Central	Beef, brisket, ribs, sausage	Dry, if served it is tomato-based	Mesquite, oak	Tangy, spicy
Texas, Eastern	Brisket, pork ribs, sausage	Thick, tomato-based	Hickory	Sweet, spicy
St. Louis, Missouri	Pork, St. Louis–style cut ribs, steaks, snoots	Very wet, thick, tomato-based	Fruit woods, cherry, apple	Caramelized, sweet, spicy

Some of the most popular meats used for barbecue are pork butt or shoulder, beef brisket, pork, beef ribs, and fowl (see page 3 for the most common cuts of beef and pork). Purchase high-quality meat with some exterior fat. If you are purchasing multiple pieces of the same cut, try to get them as close in size as possible so that they will be finished more or less at the same time. While some cooks prefer to leave all the fat on the meat, most prefer to trim much of it off. For the recipes in this book, we recommend trimming the fat down to ¼ to ½ inch or so, enough to baste and protect the meat from getting dry during the long cooking process. When cooking ribs, it is generally preferred to pull the membrane, known as silverskin, off the back of the ribs to make them less chewy and to absorb more seasonings, as shown in the photo at right.

The major difference between slow roasting and barbecue is the smoke. The product needs to be cooked slowly in the 225° to 250°F range in a contained environment with the gentle application of smoke. This can be accomplished in a gas grill, charcoal grill, pit, or smoker.

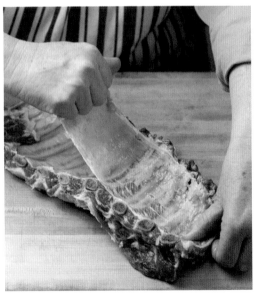

Before cooking baby back ribs or spareribs, you'll need to remove the membrane that covers the bone side of the rack, known as "silverskin." Cut a slit along the membrane at one end of the ribs to loosen the membrane. Grip the membrane firmly and peel it off in one piece.

It is best if the heat is maintained at a constant temperature, and the smoker opened as little as possible to keep the heat and smoke in the chamber. Monitoring the temperature with a dual probe thermometer will help you avoid opening the smoker. The temperature of the meat should also be closely monitored. With a probe in the meat, you can monitor the slow rise in the meat's temperature and its ultimate doneness. Gentle wisps of smoke should be exiting the chamber, so the fuel and smoke source must be closely monitored. Too

THE SMOKE RING

One quality indicator in barbecue is the "smoke ring." This is a pink or red ring around the edge of the finished product. The smoke ring is desirable, and judges in barbecue competitions want to see that the smoke ring present, but it has little to do with smoke. The smoke ring is a chemical reaction between nitrogen dioxide, produced by the burning wood, and the amino acids in the meat. The nitrogen settles on the surface of the meat and as a result a chemical process between the meat juices and the nitrogen creates the smoke ring.

The wood must be burning at a temperature exceeding 600°F in order to produce nitrogen dioxide. This is why you will not see a smoke ring on smokers that use sawdust or briquettes. They burn at a lower temperature and so do not produce nitrogen dioxide.

When this smoke ring appears on chicken or poultry, it may give the appearance that it isn't cooked enough—it is. The chicken cooks from the outside in, and this ring will be around the outside of the chicken, which cooks first. It's a good thing, and one indicator that you made good barbecue.

BARK, MR. BROWN, OR BURNT ENDS

Bark, also known as Mr. Brown, is the black, crusty, smoky, and intensely flavored outside of a barbecued pork butt or shoulder. When pulling pork, it is important to include some of the bark with each portion to provide some of this intense flavor and texture.

much smoke can overpower the product and give it a sooty, acrid flavor. A pan of water should also be added to the cooking chamber to keep it moist. When preparing your grill, always prepare it for indirect heat, as described on page 6.

Some cooks wrap aluminum foil around the meat during part of the cooking process. This holds steam inside the foil package and can lead to faster cooking and a moister product. The meat can be removed from the foil and put back into the heat to create a crispy "bark" if preferred.

Doneness can be determined by visually inspecting the meat or pulling at it to make sure it is tender. This is the case with ribs. Proper doneness can also be determined in most products with a temperature reading. The right temperature will vary between the various meats, cuts of meats, and how you plan to serve it, and is given in most of the recipes in this book.

A hallmark of barbecued meats is their complex, deep flavors. More than in braising or roasting, barbecue products are highly seasoned. They can be dry-cured, brined, rubbed with spices, or marinated before cooking, or basted with a full-flavored sauce during or after cooking. Unlike in braising or roasting, when barbecuing, the sauce is made separately from the meat, and often features sweet, spicy, and tart flavors. And of course, the smoke itself is a key component that contributes to the flavor and texture of the meat.

Smoke comes from burning wood, either by placing it directly on the coals of a charcoal grill, or in a separate box or chamber in a gas grill or smoker. There is a learning curve to applying smoke to meat. Enough smoke in the chamber is needed to complement the product, but not so much that it dominates the meat's natural flavor with a resinous or sooty flavor.

You may have heard that soaking the wood in water will generate more smoke. This is a myth! Placing a wet piece of wood on a hot fire will certainly produce some smoke, but it will also cool the fire off and cause the temperature to drop inside the chamber. Dry wood should always be used. The vents should also be set properly to control the burning embers and ensure that the wood smolders slowly rather than burning up quickly. Wrap the wood in aluminum foil or use a firebox to restrict the airflow and make the wood smoke more. There should be only gentle wisps of smoke exiting through the vent holes.

THE PLATEAU

The term "plateau" in the barbecue world refers to a point at which a barbecued or slow-roasted beef brisket or pork butt will hold at a certain temperature for a period of time. This temperature will be in the 160° to 170°F range. The meat will sit at this temperature, or may even drop a few degrees, for hours. This is an important point in the cooking process. Collagen is being dissolved and converted to liquid gelatin. This conversion creates extra moisture in the meat, and it requires more time and energy to facilitate the conversion. Be patient; the temperature will increase eventually and will continue on at a steady pace until your desired final temperature is reached, providing you with juicy, tender meat.

CHOOSING THE RIGHT WOOD FOR BARBECUING

TYPE OF WOOD	CHARACTERISTICS	FOODS TO MATCH	NOTES
Hickory	Pungent, smoky, bacon-like flavor	Pork; chicken; beef; wild game; cheese	Most widely used product
Pecan	Rich; more subtle than hickory but similar in taste	Pork; chicken; lamb; fish; cheese	Burns cool, so ideal for very-low-heat smoking
Mesquite	Sweeter, more delicate flavor than hickory	Beef; most vegetables	Tends to burn hot, so use carefully
Alder	Delicate flavor that enhances lighter meats	Salmon, swordfish, sturgeon, other fish; chicken; pork	
Oak	Forthright but pleasant flavor	Beef items like brisket; poultry; pork	Blends well with a variety of toughness/tenderness and juiciness and has medium flavor
Maple	Mildly smoky, somewhat sweet flavor	Ham, bacon; poultry; vegetables	Try mixing with corncobs
Cherry	Slightly sweet, fruity flavor	Poultry; game birds; pork	
Apple	Slightly sweet but denser fruity flavor	Beef; poultry; game birds; pork such as ham	
Peach or Pear	Slightly sweet, woodsy flavor	Poultry; game birds; pork	
Grapevines	Aromatic, similar to fruit woods	Turkey, chicken; beef	
Wine Barrel Chips	Wine and oak flavors	Beef; turkey; cheese	A flavorful novelty that smells wonderful, too
Seaweed	Tangy and smoky flavors	Lobster, crab, shrimp, mussels, clams	Wash and dry in sun before use
Herbs; spices; aromatics (bay leaves, rosemary, mint, oregano, whole nutmeg, cinnamon sticks, lemon peels, garlic, jasmine or other teas, peanut shells)		Vegetables; cheese; small pieces of meat (lighter and thin-cut meats; fish steaks and fillets; kebabs)	

Rubs, Marinades, Dry Cures, and Brines

CURING AND BRINING, BOTH FORMS OF SALTING, were historically the most popular methods of preserving meat, fish, and poultry. Today we have refrigeration and freezing and a steady supply of most meats and seafood, so cures and brines are used, along with spice rubs and marinades, for flavor only, not preservation. (These processes also lend themselves particularly well to slow roasting; see Chapter 4.)

The processes of dry rubbing, marinating, curing, and brining can all be sped up with the use of a vacuum sealer. Dry products like dry rubs and dry cures can be applied to the product, placed into a vacuum-sealable bag, and vacuum sealed. The vacuum will pull the salt and spices into the meat faster. Vacuum canisters large enough to fit your product work well with marinades and brines. Place the product into a canister, cover with the brine or marinade, and then seal using a tube that attaches the canister to the vacuum machine. When the machine goes through its vacuum cycle, much of the air is removed from the canister and the marinating process is sped up.

INGREDIENTS

Salt is the main item used in rubs, marinades, cures, and brines. Kosher salt is used for all of the recipes in this book and it's particularly important that kosher salt be used. Table salt has anti-caking agents and iodine added, and smaller cubic-shaped crystals. Kosher salt doesn't have any additives and is made up of larger irregular-shaped crystals with more surface area. Its size and shape allow it to absorb more moisture than other types of salt and makes it excellent for curing meats.

Along with the salt, you will often see sweeteners added to rubs, marinades, cures, and brines. This combination of salty and sweet provides balance in foods: Think of bacon, smoked ham, or many Asian-inspired dishes. The sweetener and the amount used will vary depending on the desired end flavor or color of the product. White sugar, honey, brown sugar, and maple syrup are only a few of the sweeteners commonly used. Not all sugars provide the same sweetening power or relative sweetness, so experiment with the types of sweeteners to see which you like best.

In terms of additional seasonings, the sky is the limit. An infinite amount of flavor profiles can be created and there are thousands of recipes for rubs, marinades, cures, and brines. This is where your creativity can come in.

RUBS

Rubs are mixtures of dry spices and herbs. The rub adds a depth of flavor and texture to the outside of the product—rubs are all about flavor! It can be as simple as salt and black pepper rubbed into a pork shoulder before roasting, or a mixture of ingredients that target a particular style or flavor profile such as Southwestern, Asian, or Latin or mild, sweet, or spicy. A rub can be dry or wet and is gently massaged into the meat. The meat can be cooked immediately or refrigerated overnight to draw more seasoning into the meat. When using a dry rub, a fresh dusting of rub should be applied before cooking. Sometimes a rub is added after the product has been cured to take advantage of both techniques. This creates another layer of flavor in the meat. There are thousands of prepackaged spice mixtures, or "rubs," available in markets and online. Freshness is the key when selecting these products. Penzeys is an excellent online purveyor of fresh, high-quality spices and herbs. You should also avoid any commercial spice mixtures that include enzymes or meat tenderizers. As a general rule, use about 1 or 2 tablespoons per pound of meat when massaging the rub into the meat.

A "dry rub" is simply a mix of dried ingredients such as salt, spices, and herbs. A "wet rub" is a dry rub mixture that is bound together with a liquid like oil, mustard, juice, or wine and is used in the same manner as a dry rub. A wet rub can also contain moist ingredients like fresh herbs, garlic, or shallots. Wet rubs tend to be less piquant than dry rubs and work particularly well with seafood.

MARINADES

Many chefs and cookbooks tout high-acid marinades for tenderizing, but today's marinades are used primarily to impart flavor. The recipes in this book use large, and often very tough, cuts of meat, and high-acid marinades cannot penetrate these large cuts deeply enough to provide much tenderizing beyond a thin layer around the surface of the meat. Certain enzymes found in packaged meat tenderizers and in tropical fruits, including pineapple, kiwi, and papaya, can also act as tenderizers. But these enzymes do not denature, or uncoil, the long strands of protein to provide tenderness, but rather cut them. This cutting of the long protein strands makes the meat mushy. For smaller cuts like steaks, the enzymes turn the meat texture to a cooked liver consistency. On larger cuts of meat, when the enzymes are applied for a longer period of time, the exterior of the meat will turn mushy. It is the cooking methods in this book—braising, barbecue, and slow roasting—that tenderize the meat during the cooking process, so additional tenderization from meat tenderizers is not needed. This is not to say that marinating meats is not a good practice, but marinating is for flavor, not tenderizing.

You should use enough marinade to completely cover the product. The amount of marinade can be reduced if the product is placed into a zip-close plastic bag or a vacuum-sealable bag. After the product is added, the marinade can be added and the excess air squeezed out before it is sealed. Never reuse a marinade.

DRY CURING

Dry curing is used in products where a lower moisture and drier texture are required, such as when smoking fish. Dry curing can be done using salt alone, but more commonly today, a cure will also include a sweetener, pepper, herbs, or citrus zest. While dry and wet rubs may also contain salt and sugar, a rub contains many more dry spices than a cure. A dry cure will add a more subtle salty or salty-sweet flavor with lighter seasonings. For the purposes of this book, we will use a dry cure when smoking seafood, as shown opposite.

A dry cure is often used to add a layer of intense flavor to fish that will be smoked, such as the trout shown here.

The cured fish will feel firm and dry to the touch even before it is cooked.

BRINING (WET CURING)

Curing meats, poultry, and fish in a salt-and-water solution is known as brining or wet curing. It provides depth in flavor, tenderness, and a moister final product. The base of a brine is salt and water, and sometimes sugar. Kosher salt is preferred because it doesn't have any additives, such as potassium iodine, dextrose, and calcium silicate, an anti-caking ingredient found in table salt. Frequently, other seasonings are included in a brine as well. Soaking in this basic solution works just fine, but often other ingredients such

as fruit juices, herbs, spices, or garlic are also added for flavor. You can tailor the flavor added by a brine by the ingredients and seasonings you use. For example, you could brine a duck breast in orange juice with orange zest, brown sugar, soy sauce, and ginger; all of these flavors match well with duck. Salt also denatures protein and makes meat tenderer. A flank steak, which is a thin cut of beef, can be chewy even if it is cut thinly against the grain after cooking. If it is allowed to cure overnight in a dry cure or brine, it will be much tenderer after being cooked. In addition, brining causes the meat to

When submerging meat in brine, be sure the meat is completely covered by the liquid.

Use a brining needle to inject brine directly into the meat.

absorb moisture, so when the product is cooked, it will be juicy and moist. Pork, "the other white meat," has been bred to be very lean. Brining leaner cuts of pork make it juicer and more flavorful after being cooked.

To prepare the brine: Bring 25 percent of the quantity of liquid to a boil with the salt, sugar, spices, and other seasonings and simmer for a few minutes to dissolve the salt and sugar and extract the flavors from the seasonings. Strain the liquid and add the remaining 75 percent of the cold liquid. The brine must be chilled to 40°F or below before adding the meat.

Then the product must be completely submerged in the brine and refrigerated (see photo, above left). If you cannot fit the product into your refrigerator, try placing the container into an ice chest and surrounding it with ice. Tall 5-gallon watercoolers, like you see at construction sites or ball games, also work well. When you make the brine, add ice to bring the total volume up to 5 gallons. There will be some ice cubes remaining that will keep the item in the safe temperature range. In cooler months you may be able to store it outside if the temperature is right. It should be held between 25°

and 40°F because the salt and sugar in the brine will allow for a lower freezing temperature.

Another way to apply brine solutions is to pump or inject them into the meat. Brining needles or flavor injectors are readily available in many stores. The cold brining solution is sucked up through a brining needle into a reservoir. The needle has several holes so that when it is inserted into the meat, the brine is pumped into all areas and depths of the meat (see photo, opposite, right). This can also be done in conjunction with submerged brining to speed up the process, especially in larger products. Pumping a 3-pound chicken with 1 cup of brine and then soaking it overnight in a brine solution will result in a very flavorful, moist, tender roast chicken.

When choosing ingredients for brines, purchase fresh, high-quality ingredients. Dried herbs and ground spices also work well, but their flavors deteriorate fairly rapidly if not stored properly or replaced regularly. So discard that bottle of granulated garlic that's been hiding in the back of your spice cabinet since you purchased the house. Purchase in small quantities and replace frequently, at least once a year. It makes a big difference in the flavor of your end product. Whole spices have a better flavor and will last longer than ground spices. Making a small investment in a mortar and pestle or small spice grinder may be worth it if you need to grind a lot of whole spices. Nowhere does freshness matter more than when using citrus juices. The content of that yellow, lemon-shaped container in your refrigerator doesn't contain a flavor remotely close to that of fresh lemon juice. Fresh citrus juices are frequently found in brines and marinades; freshly squeezed juice is the best and has an incredible impact on flavor.

Do not brine "kosher" or "enhanced" chickens. Both of these chicken products are already injected with a sodium solution. This changes the texture and flavor of the meat. It also allows the chicken to meet kosher guidelines. Placing these chickens in brine would be redundant and the final product would be too salty.

The length of time the product is in the brine depends on the size and density of the product along with the amount of brine flavor you desire. Practice will lead to fine-tuning the time to your taste. Smaller items may be brined for a couple of hours while a larger product can be brined overnight or for days. When the product is removed from the brine it needs to be rinsed, wiped dry, and allowed to air-dry before cooking. Never reuse the brine.

APPROXIMATE BRINING TIMES

ITEM	SIZE	IMMERSION ONLY	IMMERSION AND INJECTING
Whole chicken	3 lb	Overnight /12 hours	4–6 hours
Whole turkey	12–14 lb	24 hours	12 hours
Pork loin, bone in	6–8 lb	18 hours	6–8 hours
Pork loin, boneless	4–6 lb	12 hours	6 hours
Trout fillets	½ inch thick	30 minutes, dry cure	Not recommended
Pork butt, slow roast	6–8 lb, bone in	Not recommended	12–24 hours, injection only
Duck breast, Long Island	8–12 oz	2 hours	Not needed

BRINE FORMULAS

QUANTITY	WATER	KOSHER SALT	DARK BROWN SUGAR	*	WHITE GRANULATED SUGAR
5 Gallons					
Weight	40 lb	1 lb	1 lb	or	1 lb
Volume	5 gallons	1²/₃ cup	2 cups, firmly packed	or	2 cups
1 Gallon					
Weight	8 lb	3.2 oz	3.2 oz	or	3.2 oz
Volume	1 gallon	½ cup	½ cup, firmly packed		½ cup
1 Quart					
Weight	2 lb	0.8 oz	0.8 oz	or	0.8 oz
Volume	1 qt	4 tbsp	2 tbsp, firmly packed	or	2 tbsp
1 Cup					
Weight	8 oz	0.2 oz	0.2 oz	or	0.2 oz
Volume	1 cup	1 tbsp	1½ tsp	or	1½ tsp

*Use only one, either white sugar or brown sugar, based on the desired color and flavor of the brine. Using both will provide too much sweetness.

PORK RIBS: "TO BOIL OR NOT TO BOIL?" THAT IS THE QUESTION.

NO! Do not boil ribs before grilling or barbecuing. This question generates much controversy among home cooks. Many people will boil their ribs before grilling or barbecuing them, thinking that the ribs will be tenderer and cook faster. That's true, but it doesn't mean it's good. "Fall off the bone tender" is not a quality indicator. The meat should have some texture and slip off the bone easily, but it should not be falling off the bone. If it does, those ribs are overcooked.

Barbecue is a long, slow cooking process, and it's utilized to make tough cuts of meat, like ribs, tender. During that process they shrink, tenderize, and pick up a smoky flavor. Boiling provides less exposure to the smoke, so those advantages are lost. Boiling the ribs pulls flavor away from the meat. You are left with a very flavorful broth, but the flavor should be in the meat. Boiling will also remove too much fat. Fat is needed to tenderize the meat, and provide flavor and juiciness to the ribs. Dry rubs will not stick to the wet boiled ribs, which reduces the flavor potential even more.

The addition of barbecue sauce will add flavor to boiled or plain ribs, but let's face it, some barbecue sauces would taste good on cardboard. Compare boiled ribs to proper barbecued ribs and you'll taste the difference. Remember, you don't boil any other meats before grilling or barbecuing—so why would you boil pork ribs?

Use a chimney starter to light the charcoal.

Fill the water pan before you start barbecuing.

When the charcoal is hot, very carefully pour it from the chimney starter into the grill or smoker.

Place the meat inside the grill or smoker, insert a thermometer, and close the door tightly.

MASTER
TECHNIQUE

BARBECUING

81

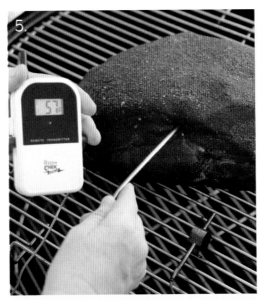

5.

Use a dual-probe thermometer to monitor the temperature of the chamber and the internal temperature of the meat.

6.

Adjust the vents of the grill or smoker to allow the proper amount of smoke to escape.

7.

The smoker should be heated to the appropriate temperature with light smoke coming out of the vents.

8.

When the meat is properly smoked, the bone should slide cleanly from the meat.

A properly smoked meat will have a black, crusty exterior, known as bark, Mr. Brown, or burnt ends (see page 68), and a pink-red smoke ring around the edge of the meat.

Eastern North Carolina Barbecued Pork Butt

1. If it has not already been removed, remove the skin of the pork butt. Trim the fat on top of the pork butt, leaving only about ¼ to ½ inch remaining. Coat the pork with a thin layer of prepared mustard and massage the mustard into the pork.

2. TO MAKE THE RUB: Combine the black pepper, paprika, sugar, salt, garlic powder, onion powder, and cayenne. Reserve 1 tablespoon of the rub mixture to make the mop. Sprinkle the remaining dry rub onto the pork and rub it into the surface of the meat. Use enough rub to completely cover the entire butt with an even layer; a good general rule is to use about 1 tablespoon of rub per pound of meat. Reserve any remaining rub for later use.

3. Wrap the pork tightly in plastic wrap and refrigerate for at least 12 hours or overnight.

4. Prepare your smoker or grill, and bring it to a temperature between 225° and 250°F with a light smoke escaping. Place a pan of water below the area where the pork will be cooked; this will keep the meat from drying out, prevent flare-ups, and help maintain the chamber temperature.

5. MEANWHILE, MAKE THE MOP: Combine the 1 tablespoon reserved rub with the vinegar, Worcestershire sauce, black pepper, salt, paprika, and cayenne. Set the mop aside.

One 6- to 8-lb Boston butt, bone in

¼ cup prepared yellow mustard

RUB

¼ cup freshly cracked black pepper

¼ cup paprika, preferably smoked Spanish paprika (see Chef's Notes)

¼ cup packed brown sugar

2 tbsp kosher salt

1 tsp garlic powder

1 tsp onion powder

1 tsp cayenne pepper

MOP

1 tbsp rub mixture

2 cups apple cider vinegar

1 tbsp Worcestershire sauce

1 tbsp freshly cracked black pepper

1 tbsp kosher salt

1 tbsp paprika, preferably smoked Spanish paprika

1 tsp cayenne pepper

LOW AND SLOW

6. Remove the pork from the refrigerator, and sprinkle it with a little more rub to dry the surface. Allow the pork to sit at room temperature for 30 minutes while the smoker or grill is heating.

7. Place the pork into the smoker or grill. Maintain a temperature between 225° and 250°F for the duration of the cooking. The best way to monitor temperature is by using two thermometers or one thermometer with two temperature probes. One thermometer will monitor the chamber temperature and the other will monitor the internal temperature of the meat. To help maintain the proper temperature, try to avoid unnecessarily opening the smoker or grill; it's best to try to go without opening it for an hour or so at a time. Each time you open the cooking unit, heat is lost and the cooking time is extended.

VINEGAR SAUCE

2 cups apple cider vinegar

2 tbsp packed brown sugar

2 tsp kosher salt

1 tsp freshly cracked black pepper

1 tsp crushed red pepper flakes

8. Each time you open the chamber, turn the pork and baste it with the mop to provide flavor and to keep the surface of the pork moist during the lengthy cooking process. While the chamber is open, also check the temperature. If the heat is dropping, add more fuel or smoking chips. If the heat is too high, close the vents, or refill the water pan if it has gone dry. (Keeping the water pan from drying out is vital to maintaining temperature and the proper moist cooking environment.)

9. **WHILE THE PORK IS COOKING, MAKE THE VINEGAR SAUCE:** Combine the vinegar, sugar, salt, black pepper, and red pepper flakes. Set the sauce aside to allow the flavors to infuse.

10. Plan to cook the pork for about 1½ hours per pound; you may want to give yourself an extra 2 hours if you are on a mealtime deadline. An 8-pound pork butt will take 10 to 12 hours to cook. It may stick and plateau for hours (see page 70); this is normal. Don't try to rush it. Increasing the temperature will negatively impact the quality of the finished meat. When the pork reaches an internal temperature of 193°F, remove it from the chamber and allow it to rest for 20 to 30 minutes.

11. Once it is cool enough to handle, "pull" or chop the pork into pieces: Pull the pork apart with two forks or your fingers, or chop it using a knife. Remove any large pieces of fat that remain, and discard them. Make sure that you mix the pork well and have the "bark" (see page 68) distributed evenly throughout the meat.

12. Dress the pork to taste with the vinegar sauce. Most, if not all, of the sauce will be required. The meat is also excellent for pulled pork sandwiches; serve on sliced soft white bread or a soft hamburger bun with coleslaw as described on page 26.

Smoked Spanish paprika, or pimentón, is preferred because the peppers are smoked over an oak fire, which gives it a smokier flavor than that of regular paprika. If it is not available, be sure to use a good-quality sweet paprika.

This recipe has a lot of fresh cracked black pepper in it. Try it as-is before deciding to reduce the amount, because you'll find that it's not an excessive amount of heat. It gets most of its heat and flavor from a delayed palate reaction to the black pepper. The initial heat will come from the cayenne and then it will finish with the black pepper. If you would like the dish to be spicier, increase the amount of cayenne.

Pig's Ear BBQ Pork Butt

Pig's Ear is the section of Lincoln, New Hampshire where I grew up. This recipe is the amalgamation of a variety of different recipes that I have tested over the years. It is a little more complicated than the Braised Pulled Pork Barbecue Sandwiches with Coleslaw (page 25). While that recipe is bold, in-your-face spicy, and acidic, this recipe features a more complex layering of flavors that gives it depth.

1. Rinse the pork with cool water and dry thoroughly. Trim any excess fat from the pork, leaving a ¼-inch layer.

2. TO MAKE THE BRINE: Combine the sugar, salt, garlic powder, cider, water, and Worcestershire sauce and stir until the salt and sugar are dissolved. Using a brining needle or injector, inject the brine evenly around the pork butt, being sure to inject at varying depths. Use all of the brine mixture.

3. TO MAKE THE DRY RUB: Combine the chili powder, sweet paprika, smoked paprika, sugar, salt, black pepper, onion powder, garlic powder, Old Bay, and red pepper flakes.

4. Rub the prepared yellow mustard evenly onto the pork butt, and sprinkle the pork with the dry rub. (The general rule is ½ ounce of dry rub per pound of pork.) Gently rub the dry rub into the pork, adding more rub as needed. Wrap the pork butt in plastic wrap and refrigerate for 2 hours or overnight. Reserve any remaining rub.

One 8- to 10-lb pork butt, bone in

BRINE

2 tbsp packed dark brown sugar

2 tbsp kosher salt

1 tsp garlic powder

1 cup apple cider

1 cup water

1 tbsp Worcestershire sauce

DRY RUB

½ cup chili powder

¼ cup sweet paprika

¼ cup smoked Spanish paprika

2 tbsp packed dark brown sugar

2 tbsp kosher salt

1 tbsp freshly cracked black pepper

(continued)

5. To make the mist: Combine the apple cider and vinegar in a food-grade spray bottle. Alternatively, the mist can be mixed in a bowl and brushed on with a brush or mop.

6. An hour before cooking, set up your smoker or charcoal or gas grill and remove the pork from the refrigerator. Unwrap the pork and allow it to air-dry. If the pork is not dry when it's time to put it into the cooking unit, sprinkle it with a little of the reserved dry rub.

7. Bring the smoker to a temperature between 225° and 250°F, fill the water pan, and develop a light smoke. Insert a probe thermometer into the center of the pork, being careful not to place it in a fat pocket or near a bone. Place the pork into the smoking unit. This will cool the unit off, so it may require some adjustments to get the temperature to settle back in the 225° to 250°F range. Try to avoid unnecessarily opening the smoker; it's best to try to go without opening it for an hour or so at a time. Each time you open the cooking unit, heat is lost and the cooking time is extended. When it is necessary to open the smoker, try to do everything at once: add fuel, add smoking material, and check the water pan. (Keeping the water pan from drying out is vital to maintaining temperature and the proper moist cooking environment.) The pork will take 10 to 14 hours to cook. When you have

1 tbsp onion powder

1 tbsp garlic powder

1 tsp Old Bay Seasoning

1 tsp crushed red pepper flakes

½ cup prepared yellow mustard

MIST

2 cups apple cider

2 cups apple cider vinegar

GLAZE

½ cup apple jelly

¼ cup apple cider

¼ cup apple cider vinegar

¼ cup honey

½ cup packed dark brown sugar

1½ tsp dry mustard powder

¼ tsp crushed red pepper flakes

to open the smoker, take advantage of the opportunity to spray the pork with the mist. This will keep the surface of the pork moist and provide flavor during the lengthy cooking process.

8. The pork will plateau when its internal temperature reaches the 163°F range (see page 70). It may stick at this temperature for hours, so be patient. The plateau will eventually release, and then the temperature will rise fairly quickly. When the pork has reached 195°F, remove it from the smoker, wrap it in plastic wrap, and allow it to rest for 1 hour. The temperature will continue to rise, reaching 205° to 210°F, which is desirable.

9. MEANWHILE, MAKE THE GLAZE: Combine the jelly, cider, vinegar, honey, sugar, mustard powder, and red pepper flakes. Refrigerate the mixture to thicken it.

10. When the pork has rested, slather the glaze evenly over the pork and place it back into the smoker. Smoke until the glaze mixture has cooked and has given the pork a shiny appearance, about 30 minutes. Remove the pork from the smoker and allow it to rest for 30 minutes.

11. At this point the pork can be pulled or sliced to be eaten on its own (as is or with the sauce of your liking), or used to make pulled pork sandwiches, Barbecued Pulled Pork Pizza (page 95), or other dish.

Barbecued Pork Butt Ravioli

MAKES 4 SERVINGS

This combination may seem unusual, but the smoky flavor of the pork works well with the tomato sauce and pasta. It's also a great way to utilize leftover pork butt or beef brisket. This recipe will produce four large ravioli per serving, suitable for a pasta course or appetizer.

1. In a large bowl, combine the pork with the chili powder and cayenne.

2. Heat the oil in a sauté pan over medium heat. Add the garlic and jalapeño, and sauté until aromatic, about 1 minute. Turn off the heat and stir in the chopped oregano. Immediately add to the pork mixture and stir to combine. If necessary, season with salt. Set the filling mixture aside to cool.

3. Using a pasta machine or rolling pin, roll out the pasta dough into thin sheets, about 1⁄16 inch thick. Cover the sheets with plastic wrap while you work to keep them from drying out.

4. Cut thirty-two 2-inch rounds from the sheets, and brush the edge of each round very lightly with water. Place 2 teaspoons of filling in the center of 16 of the rounds, and cover each of these with another round of dough.

5. Press lightly around the edge of each ravioli to remove any air between the two pasta circles and to stick the dough together.

1 cup coarsely chopped Eastern North Carolina Barbecued Pork Butt (page 84) or other cooked pork butt

1 tsp sweet chili powder

Pinch of cayenne pepper

1 tsp vegetable oil

4 garlic cloves, minced

1 tsp finely diced jalapeño

½ tsp chopped oregano, plus 1 tbsp oregano leaves

Kosher salt, as needed

1 lb Fresh Pasta dough (page 184)

1½ cups Tomato Sauce (page 227), warm

6. Crimp around the edge of each ravioli with a fork to make a tight seal. You may want to trim the ravioli using the same cutter you used to cut the rounds of dough. As you assemble the ravioli, place them on a baking sheet in a single layer and cover with plastic wrap; do not stack them.

7. In a large pot, bring a gallon of salted water to a boil over high heat. Add the ravioli and boil until tender, about 5 minutes; drain.

8. To serve, divide the ravioli and tomato sauce among four serving bowls or plates, and garnish with the oregano leaves.

If desired and available, you can fill and cut the ravioli using a ravioli board—it's much faster.

BARBECUING

Barbecued Pulled Pork Pizza

MAKES TWO 12-INCH PIZZAS

Leftover pulled pork can be used to make a very tasty and unique pizza. A little pork (about 1½ cups) is enough for 4 to 5 portions.

1. TO MAKE THE DOUGH: Combine the bread flour, semolina flour, and yeast in the bowl of a stand mixer fitted with the dough hook attachment. Add the water, olive oil, and salt and mix on low speed for 2 minutes. Increase the speed to medium and knead until the dough is quite elastic but still a little sticky, about 4 minutes.

2. Transfer the dough to a lightly oiled bowl, turn to coat with the oil, cover with plastic wrap or a damp towel, and let rise in a warm place until nearly doubled in size, about 30 minutes.

3. Fold the dough gently, cover, and let rest until relaxed, 15 to 20 minutes. Cut the dough into 2 equal pieces and round them into smooth balls. Cover the balls of dough and let rest another 15 to 20 minutes.

4. Press each ball of dough into a 12-inch disk.

5. Place a pizza stone on the middle shelf of the oven and preheat the oven to 500°F, or prepare the grill (see Chef's Notes).

6. TO MAKE THE TOPPINGS: Heat the oil in a sauté pan over medium heat. Add the onion and cook slowly over medium heat until wilted, about 5 minutes. This will prevent the onions from burning in the oven.

SEMOLINA PIZZA DOUGH

3½ cups bread flour, plus more as needed

½ cup semolina or durum flour

1½ tsp active dry yeast

1½ cups room-temperature water

3 tbsp olive oil, plus more as needed

2 tsp kosher salt

TOPPINGS

1 tbsp olive oil

1 cup thinly sliced red onion

1 cup Classic Barbecue Sauce (page 216), or your favorite barbecue sauce

1½ cups pulled pork (see page 84, 89; see Chef's Notes)

2 cups sharp cheddar cheese

½ tsp crushed red pepper flakes (optional)

Cornmeal, for dusting

¼ cup cilantro, whole leaves with stems removed (optional)

BARBECUING

95

7. Spread ½ cup of the barbecue sauce onto one of the two pizza dough crusts. Scatter ¾ cup of the pulled pork, 1 cup of the cheese, and ½ cup of the onions over the barbecue sauce. Sprinkle with some red pepper flakes if using.

8. Dust the pizza stone with cornmeal and place the pizza onto the preheated stone. Bake until the cheese starts to brown and get bubbly, about 10 minutes. While the first pizza is baking, prepare the second pizza, using the remaining ingredients. When the first pizza comes out of the oven, replace it with the second pizza and bake it in the same way.

9. As the pizzas come out of the oven, sprinkle with the cilantro, if desired, and let cool for 5 minutes before cutting and serving. Slice each pizza into 6 pieces.

Although this is an excellent pizza dough, premade pizza dough or prebaked pizza crusts are available in supermarkets and may be substituted for the semolina crust in this recipe. If using premade dough, use 12 ounces of pizza dough per pizza. If using a prebaked or parbaked crust, lower the oven temperature to 425°F.

Either of the barbecued pork butt recipes will work well in this recipe. You could also use leftover beef brisket (page 104).

Using a charcoal grill will give your pizza a wood-fired flavor and character. To use this method, ignite about 3 pounds of charcoal and let it burn in a pile in the grill. When the coals are mostly white hot, spread them out around the circumference of the grill and place the rack back in the grill. Place the pizza stone onto the rack, and cover with all vents open. Let the grill preheat to 500°F, then follow the same process as described at left.

Smoke-Roasted Sirloin of Beef

Have you ever noticed how the roast beef sliced at a deli is rare to medium-rare almost to the very edge of the meat? That is the result of low-temperature, slow cooking. Generally you would roast a very tender cut of meat like beef sirloin at a higher temperature, but occasionally such meats, like prime rib and turkey, are slow roasted. This technique provides very little shrinkage and a better retention of natural juices. Serve the sirloin with Watercress Salad with Horseradish Vinaigrette (page 199) and Tomato Salsa (page 229), Classic Barbecue Sauce (page 216), or Creamy Horseradish Sauce (page 223).

1. Trim the top of the sirloin of excess fat, leaving only about a ¼-inch layer on top. You may see some very heavy connective tissue on the thick side of the sirloin as well. If so, place the tip of your knife under it and slice off as much of the tissue as you can.

2. TO MAKE THE DRY RUB: Combine the sugar, paprika, salt, black pepper, cumin, chili powder, garlic powder, onion powder, and cayenne and mix well to evenly distribute the spices.

3. Rub the dry rub all over the sirloin strip and allow it to rest for 15 minutes. You may not need all of the dry rub mixture, but make sure that the entire sirloin is covered.

4. Meanwhile, prepare the smoker, charcoal grill, gas grill, or oven for barbecuing. If using an oven, set the temperature to 250°F. If using a smoker or grill, bring the temperature to 250°F, fill the water pan, and

One 4-lb sirloin strip roast

DRY RUB

¼ cup sugar

¼ cup sweet paprika

3 tbsp kosher salt

2 tbsp freshly cracked black pepper

2 tbsp ground cumin

2 tbsp chili powder

1 tbsp garlic powder

1 tbsp onion powder

1 tbsp cayenne pepper

develop a light smoke. It's important that the temperature stays in the 225° to 250°F range with a small amount of light smoke escaping.

See page 6 for information on adding a smoker box to a charcoal or gas grill.

5. Place the sirloin in the cooking unit. This will cool the unit off, so it may require some time and adjustments to bring the temperature back to the 225° to 250°F range. Cook until the sirloin reaches an internal temperature of 120° to 125°F for medium-rare, about 2 hours. Remove the sirloin from the cooking unit, and let it rest for 20 minutes to allow the juices to redistribute before slicing.

6. Slice the sirloin against the grain to the desired thickness, and serve.

Asian Glazed Flank Steak

MAKES 6 SERVINGS

This salty, sweet, and spicy glaze has a touch of smoke that works well with the deep, rich flavor of the beef. Be sure to marinate the meat for at least 12 hours to allow the sodium content of the soy sauce to cure and tenderize the meat.

1. Trim any excess fat from the flank steak.

2. TO MAKE THE MARINADE: Combine the soy sauce, honey, mirin, sesame oil, and Sriracha in a zip-close plastic bag. Add the flank steaks to the bag and seal tightly, squeezing out as much air as possible. If you have a vacuum sealer, place the ingredients in vacuum-sealable bag, vacuum, and seal. Place the bag in the refrigerator overnight or for up to 24 hours to marinate.

3. Remove the flank steaks from the bag, drain off and reserve the excess marinade, and reserve the steaks at room temperature.

4. Transfer the marinade to a small saucepan and bring to a boil over high heat. Reduce the heat and allow the marinade to simmer until it has reduced by one-third, about 5 minutes. Remove from the heat and allow to cool.

5. Meanwhile, prepare the smoker, charcoal grill, or gas grill, or preheat the oven. If using a smoker or grill, bring the temperature to 250°F, fill the water pan, and develop a light smoke. It's important that the temperature stays in the 225° to 250°F range with a small amount of light smoke escaping. If using the oven method, preheat the oven to 250°F.

2 flank steaks (3 to 3½ lb total)

MARINADE

½ cup soy sauce

¼ cup honey

¼ cup mirin

2 tbsp dark sesame oil

1 tsp Sriracha sauce

6. Baste the flank steaks with the marinade and place them into the cooking unit. This will cool the unit so it may require some time and adjustments to bring the temperature back to the 225° to 250°F range. Cook, basting the steaks with the marinade every 20 minutes, until the steaks reach an internal temperature of 130°F for medium-rare, 1 to 1½ hours. Remove the flank steaks from the cooking unit, and let rest for 20 minutes to allow the juices to redistribute before slicing. If you would like a deeper color, place the flank steaks into a 450°F oven for 5 minutes once they are removed from the cooking unit.

7. Cut the steaks against the grain into slices, ¼ inch or thinner, and serve.

Beef Jerky

MAKES ABOUT ½ LB (ABOUT 10 SERVINGS)

Drying beef was once a necessity for preserving meat. Today, dried beef is enjoyed as a delicious snack food. This smoked version is very simple to make, but it also works well to dehydrate the beef in a low-temperature oven or in a dehydrator if you prefer not to have a smoky flavor or to go through the extra effort of smoking it. Once dry, this jerky will keep for up to three months, stored in an airtight container in a cool, dry place.

1. Trim the beef of any excess fat. Place the beef in a zip-close plastic bag and freeze for 1 to 2 hours in order to firm the meat, which will make it easier to slice.

2. If using flank steak, thinly slice the meat across the grain into strips no larger than ¼ inch thick. Flank steak is a thin, lean cut of meat that is easier to cut against the grain, which makes the jerky more tender. If using round roast, slice the meat with the grain into 2-inch-wide strips, then cut those strips against the grain into ¼-inch-thick slices.

3. **TO MAKE THE MARINADE:** Combine the Worcestershire sauce, soy sauce, sugar, black pepper, onion powder, garlic powder, and red pepper flakes. Mix well and place in a zip-close plastic bag.

4. Add the beef strips to the marinade, seal the bag tightly, and refrigerate for 6 to 12 hours. Remove the meat from the marinade and pat it with paper towels to remove any excess liquid.

2 lb flank steak or lean beef round roast

MARINADE

⅔ cup Worcestershire sauce

⅔ cup soy sauce

1 tbsp packed brown sugar

2 tsp freshly ground black pepper

2 tsp onion powder

1 tsp garlic powder

1 tsp crushed red pepper flakes

5. Spray the grill racks with nonstick cooking spray. Arrange the meat on the racks and place on the grill over indirect heat (page 6) or inside a smoker set to very low heat (150°F or under). Do not fill the water pan. Smoke the meat under low smoke for 2 hours. The meat may also be dehydrated in a 150°F oven or food dehydrator. The jerky will not have the smoky flavor, but the preparation will be easier and the final product will still be very tasty.

6. If using the grill or smoker, after 2 hours, transfer the meat from the grill or smoking unit to a 150°F oven. If you have a convection oven with a drying option, that works well for this recipe.

7. Since the type of meat, thickness of the slices, temperatures, and humidity levels can vary, it is difficult to determine exactly how long the meat will take to dry. It could take as little as 2 hours, or up to 4 or more hours. Taste the jerky to assure that it is completely dry and has a leathery but chewable texture before removing it from the oven. Allow the finished jerky to cool at room temperature, then transfer it to an airtight container and store in a cool, dry place for up to 3 months.

Barbecued Beef Brisket

This procedure is a little different from the other barbecue processes due to the nature of the cut; brisket is a tough cut of meat because it is a muscle that holds 60 percent of the steer's standing weight. This method will reduce the cooking time and will provide the tenderest, moistest result. Per pound of brisket, inject 2 tablespoons broth and rub with 2 tablespoons of dry rub. If desired, serve the brisket with Whipped Potatoes (page 173) or Oven-Roasted Potatoes (page 172), Boston Baked Beans (page 200), or Roasted Root Vegetables (page 170).

1. Using a sharp knife, remove all but ¼ inch of fat from the top of the brisket. If there is any other excess fat or silverskin, remove that as well; if using a whole brisket, do not remove the fat between the two muscles.

2. Using an injection needle, inject the brisket with ¾ cup of the broth. Be sure to inject the broth evenly around the brisket at various depths. Rub the brisket first with the mustard and then with the dry rub. Refrigerate the brisket for at least 2 hours or overnight. The time in the refrigerator will turn the rub into a paste, which will then become the "bark" on the brisket after it has cooked (see page 68). Remove the brisket from the refrigerator 1 hour before cooking.

3. Prepare the smoker (see Chef's Notes). When the smoker has settled at a temperature between 250° and 275°F (just below 275°F is best) with a gentle stream of smoke exiting the vents, place the brisket, fat side up, into the smoker. Maintain the temperature for the duration of cooking by adjusting

One 6-lb beef brisket (see Chef's Notes)

1¼ cups beef broth

¼ cup prepared yellow mustard

¾ cup Dry Rub for Beef (page 214)

Tangy Barbecue Sauce (page 217), as needed

LOW AND SLOW

the vents and adding more fuel as necessary. If desired, place a pan of water below the area where the brisket will be cooked to keep the meat from drying out, to prevent flare-ups, and to help moderate the chamber temperature. Do not open the smoker any more than you need to; every time you open the chamber, heat escapes and the cooking time is extended. Resist the urge to take a peek, and try to go 1 to 1½ hours without opening it. Every time you open the chamber to view the brisket, check and add smoking material, fuel, and water if needed.

4. Plan to cook the brisket for about 1½ hours per pound (but it's best to give yourself an hour or two of padding if you have a mealtime deadline, as the cooking time can vary). The 6-pound brisket in this recipe should take about 10 hours to cook. It may stick and plateau for hours (see page 70); this is normal. Don't rush it. Increasing the temperature will negatively impact the quality of the finished meat.

5. When the brisket breaks away from the plateau and reaches 180°F, remove the brisket from the chamber and place it on a double layer of aluminum foil. Form the foil around the brisket, leaving just enough space to pour in the broth. Pour the remaining ½ cup broth over the brisket, and wrap it up tightly with the foil.

6. With the sealed side up, place the foil-wrapped brisket back into the chamber. Insert a meat probe into the top of the brisket, making sure that it is deep enough to reach down to the center of the brisket. Smoke is not important now as it cannot penetrate the foil, but dial back the heat to try to keep the chamber about 200°F.

7. When the brisket reaches an internal temperature of 190°F, remove it from the chamber and place it into an ice chest or insulated box with a cover and allow the meat to rest for 1 to 2 hours. During this time, the cooking juices and beef broth will redistribute throughout the meat, making it exceptionally juicy.

8. To serve, unwrap the brisket and reserve any juices in the foil package. The brisket is made up of two muscles. One of the muscles lies with the grain in the opposite direction from the other. These muscles are separated by a thick layer of fat. If using a whole brisket, separate the two muscles by cutting through the fat layer in between the muscles, remove any remaining fat, and slice the meat against the grain. The juices can be served with the meat, added to the barbecue sauce, or reserved to reheat with any leftovers. Serve the meat with the barbecue sauce.

If you are going to feed a crowd of 12 to 15 people, cook a whole 13- to 15-pound brisket. For a smaller crowd, brisket also comes split in half; you'll find it sold as a "flat cut" or a "point cut" (see page 4). The flat cut is leaner and best used for braising, while the point cut is best for barbecuing. The point cut is a thicker, fattier cut, containing a layer of fat between two muscles; it can be easily identified by its pointy shape. These cuts are usually in the 6-pound range.

See page 6 for information on adding a smoker box to a charcoal or gas grill.

See page 12 for information on probe thermometers.

LOW AND SLOW

Memphis-Style Dry Ribs

Memphis-style ribs are coated with a dry rub and barbecued. The "dry ribs" are then served without any sauce or glaze on the ribs. I recommend serving at least two dipping sauces on the side. Generally these dipping sauces will be thin with sweet or sweet-and-sour flavor profiles.

1. Rinse the ribs under cool running water and dry them thoroughly with paper towels. Trim any excess fat from the meat side and edges of the ribs. On the bone side, grasp the silverskin (see Chef's Notes) from the inside of the ribs and pull it off.

2. TO MAKE THE DRY RUB: Combine the sugar, pepper, salt, paprika, chili powder, onion powder, garlic powder, thyme, oregano, coriander seeds, celery seeds, cumin seeds, and mustard powder in a bowl.

3. Sprinkle 1 tablespoon of the dry rub onto each side of each of the racks of ribs, rubbing it into the meat lightly and evenly. (Two tablespoons are required per rack.) Reserve any extra dry rub. Stack the racks on top of each other and wrap tightly in plastic wrap. Refrigerate for at least 4 hours or overnight; overnight is best.

4. One hour before cooking, remove the ribs from the refrigerator, unwrap, and allow to warm slightly at room temperature before cooking. If they are wet after refrigeration, the ribs can be sprinkled lightly with a little of the reserved dry rub.

3 full racks pork ribs, St. Louis–style cut (8 to 10 lb; ½ rack per person)

DRY RUB

¼ cup packed dark brown sugar

1 tbsp freshly cracked black pepper

1 tbsp kosher salt

2 tbsp smoked Spanish paprika

2 tbsp mild chili powder

1 tbsp onion powder

2 tsp garlic powder

2 tsp dried whole thyme leaves (see Chef's Notes)

1 tsp dried oregano, whole or flaked (see Chef's Notes)

2 tsp whole coriander seeds (see Chef's Notes)

2 tsp whole celery seeds (see Chef's Notes)

1 tsp whole cumin seeds (see Chef's Notes)

1 tsp dry mustard powder

(continued)

5. **To make the mist:** Combine the vinegar with the water in a food-grade spray bottle. Alternatively, the mist can be mixed in a bowl and brushed on with a brush or mop.

6. Prepare the smoker or grill for barbecuing. Bring the temperature to 225° to 250°F, fill the water pan, and develop a light smoke. It's important to maintain the proper temperature, so the smoker temperature should stay in the 225° to 250°F range with a small amount of light smoke escaping. Place the pork in the smoking unit. This will cool the unit off, so it may require some adjustments to get the temperature to settle back in the 225° to 250°F range.

7. Try to avoid unnecessarily opening the smoker; it's best to try to go without opening it for an hour or so at a time. Each time you open the cooking unit heat is lost and the cooking time is extended. When it is necessary to open the smoker, try to do everything at once: add fuel, add smoking material, and check the water pan. (Keeping the water pan from drying out is vital to maintaining temperature and keeping the proper moist cooking environment.) When you have to open the smoker, also take advantage of the opportunity to spray the pork with the mist mixture. This will keep the surface of the pork moist and provide flavor during the lengthy cooking process.

MIST

1 cup distilled vinegar

1 cup water

1 cup each of Jack Black Barbecue Sauce (page 218) and Classic Barbecue Sauce (page 216), thinned with water if necessary, or your desired variety and style of dipping sauces

8. When the meat starts to pull down ¼ to ½ inch on the bone, mist the ribs one more time and start checking for tenderness. Cook until the ribs are fork-tender, 3 to 5 hours; remember that each rack may take a different amount of time to cook. Remove the ribs from the smoker, and allow them to rest for 10 minutes before slicing. Slice the racks into individual ribs or double ribs, cutting down the center of the meat between each of the ribs. They will generally split apart easily.

9. Serve the ribs with the barbecue sauces on the side.

If substituting a ground herb or spice for whole or flaked, use only half the amount listed in the ingredient list.

Silverskin is a thin, tough membrane that covers the full length of ribs on the back, or bone, side (see page 67). Some cooks prefer to leave this membrane on, but most cooks prefer to remove it. Because it is so tough, silverskin can prevent seasoning and smoke from penetrating into the meat.

Slow cooking in an oven can produce decent ribs, but of course they will not have that smoke flavor. If using the oven method, set the temperature between 225° and 250°F.

Rib racks allow you to fit more ribs in a smaller space because they are oriented vertically.

Smoked Pork Belly

Pork belly is literally the belly portion of the pig. It's where bacon comes from, and like bacon, it is a delicious piece of meat. While it cooks, the fat renders from the belly and naturally bastes the strips of tender meat. Pair it with Carolina Mustard Sauce (page 219), or serve it with steamed Chinese white sandwich buns and Asian-Style Dipping Sauce (page 221).

1. TO MAKE THE MARINADE: Combine the vinegar, bourbon, honey, soy sauce, mustard, ginger, red pepper flakes, black pepper, garlic powder, and onion powder in a 1-gallon zip-close plastic bag. Place the pork into the bag, squeeze out all excess air, and seal the bag. Place in the refrigerator for at least 12 hours or overnight, turning the bag over periodically.

2. Remove the pork from the refrigerator 1 hour before cooking. Remove the pork from the bag, and transfer the marinade to a small saucepan.

3. Meanwhile, prepare the smoker, grill, or oven: Bring the temperature to 225° to 250°F, fill the water pan, and develop a light smoke. It's important to maintain the proper temperature, so the smoker temperature should stay in the 225° to 250°F range with a small amount of light smoke escaping. Place the pork in the smoking unit. This will cool the unit off, so it may require some adjustments to get the temperature to settle back in the 225° to 250°F range.

MARINADE

½ cup apple cider vinegar

¼ cup Jack Daniels bourbon or other whiskey

¼ cup honey

2 tbsp soy sauce

1 tbsp grainy mustard

1½ tsp ground ginger

1 tsp crushed red pepper flakes

1 tsp freshly cracked black pepper

1 tsp garlic powder

1 tsp onion powder

One 2½-lb pork belly, skin removed, cut into 3- to 4-inch rectangular strips

LOW AND SLOW

4. While the pork is cooking, bring the marinade to a boil over high heat. Reduce the heat to establish a simmer, and simmer for 3 minutes. Remove the pan from the heat. Baste the pork belly periodically with the marinade.

5. Try to avoid unnecessarily opening the smoker; it's best to try to go without opening it for an hour or so at a time. Each time you open the cooking unit heat is lost and the cooking time gets extended. When it is necessary to open the smoker, try to do everything at once: add fuel, add smoking material, baste the pork belly, and check the water pan. (Keeping the water pan from drying out is vital to maintaining temperature and keeping the proper moist cooking environment.) Cook until the pork belly reaches an internal temperature of 195°F, 4 to 5 hours. Remove the pork from the smoker and allow to rest for 15 minutes.

6. To serve, slice the pork into pieces ¼ to ½ inch thick and 3 or 4 inches long.

Smoke-Roasted Pork Loin with Smoked Applesauce

MAKES 6 SERVINGS

Since pork loin is one of the tenderest cuts of pork, it is not necessary to slow cook it; however, today's hogs are being bred to be so low in fat that the loin can still benefit from a low, slow cooking process. Boston Baked Beans (page 200), Braised Red Cabbage (page 166), Roasted Root Vegetables (page 170), Coleslaw (page 163), or Warm German Potato Salad (page 176) go well with this dish.

1. To make the brine: Prepare the brine as described on page 76, and add the brown sugar, cinnamon, bay leaves, and peppercorns. Once the brine has chilled, use an injection needle to inject ¾ cup of brine into the pork. Place the pork into the remaining brine, and refrigerate for 6 hours. Alternatively, you can skip the injection process, and brine the pork for 12 hours or overnight in the refrigerator.

2. Two hours before cooking, remove the pork from the brine, rinse under cool running water, and place it back in the refrigerator, uncovered, to air-dry for 1 hour. One hour before cooking, remove the pork from the refrigerator and allow to warm slightly, uncovered, at room temperature.

3. Set up your smoker or charcoal or gas grill. Bring the temperature to 275° to 300°F and develop a light smoke. Insert a probe thermometer into the center of the pork, and place the pork in the smoking unit. Placing the pork into the unit will cool it off, so the unit may require some time and adjustments for the

BRINE

2 qt basic brine (see chart, page 79)

¼ cup firmly packed brown sugar

1 tsp ground cinnamon

2 bay leaves

8 whole black peppercorns

One 2½-lb, boneless, center-cut, pork loin

6 Granny Smith apples, peeled, cored, and quartered

1 cup apple cider or apple juice, plus more as needed

1 tbsp apple cider vinegar

¼ cup granulated sugar, plus more as needed

½ tsp ground cinnamon, plus more as needed

¼ tsp freshly grated nutmeg, plus more as needed

temperature to settle in the 275° to 300°F range. It's very important to maintain this temperature range with a light smoke exiting the chamber.

4. While the pork is cooking, place the apples into the chamber on a grill or rack and smoke them for 30 to 35 minutes. Transfer the smoked apples to a 2-quart sauce pot and add the apple cider or juice, vinegar, sugar, cinnamon, and nutmeg. Cover the pot and gently simmer over low heat until the apples are very tender, about 15 minutes. Transfer the mixture to a blender and purée until smooth. At this point the apples should be the consistency of a medium-thick sauce; if necessary, adjust the consistency with some apple juice. This will be served as a sauce over or under the meat and not a side dish. Adjust the seasoning of the sauce with additional sugar, cinnamon, and nutmeg as needed.

5. Cook the pork until it has reached an internal temperature of 145°F, about 2 hours. Remove the pork from the unit. Cover the pork loosely with aluminum foil and allow it to rest for 20 minutes before carving. Reheat the applesauce if necessary before serving with the pork loin.

6. To serve, carve the pork against the grain into ¼-inch-thick slices, arrange the slices on a platter, and cover with the applesauce.

BARBECUING

Kansas City Wet-Style Barbecue Pork Spareribs

These are wet, sticky, messy ribs that are beautifully glazed with the sauce during cooking. Additional sauce may be served on the side.

1. Rinse the ribs under cool running water and dry them thoroughly. Trim any excess fat from the meat side of the ribs. On the bone side, grasp the silverskin (see Chef's Notes) from the inside of the ribs and pull it off. Slather all sides of the ribs with the prepared mustard; this will help the dry rub stick better.

2. TO MAKE THE DRY RUB: Combine the sugar, onion powder, mustard powder, garlic powder, salt, paprika, cinnamon, thyme, and cayenne in a bowl. Rub the mixture evenly onto all sides of the ribs. Generally ½ ounce of rub is adequate per 1 pound of ribs. Reserve any extra dry rub.

3. Allow the ribs to sit at room temperature for at least 30 minutes, or wrap the ribs in plastic wrap and refrigerate overnight. Overnight is best, but then the ribs will need to be removed from the refrigerator and allowed to warm slightly at room temperature before placing them in the cooker. If the ribs are wet after refrigeration, they can be sprinkled with a little of the reserved dry rub.

4. TO MAKE THE MIST: Combine the apple juice, vinegar, and Worcestershire sauce in a food-grade spray bottle. Alternatively, the mist can be brushed on with a brush or mop. Reserve.

6 to 8 lb pork spareribs, baby back or St. Louis–style cut

1 cup prepared yellow mustard

DRY RUB

½ cup packed brown sugar

¼ cup onion powder

¼ cup dry mustard powder

3 tbsp plus ½ tsp garlic powder

2 tbsp kosher salt

1 tbsp smoked Spanish paprika

2 tsp ground cinnamon

1 tsp dried thyme

½ tsp cayenne pepper

MIST

1½ cups apple juice

½ cup apple cider vinegar

2 tbsp Worcestershire sauce

1 qt prepared barbecue sauce

5. Prepare the smoker or grill for barbecuing: Bring the temperature to 225° to 250°F, fill the water pan, and develop a light smoke. It's very important to maintain the proper temperature, so keep the smoker temperature in the 225° to 250°F range with a small amount of light smoke escaping. Place the pork in the smoking unit. This will cool the unit off, so it may require some adjustments to get the temperature to settle back in the 225° to 250°F range.

6. Try to avoid unnecessarily opening the smoker; it's best to try to go without opening it for an hour or so at a time. Each time you open the cooking unit heat is lost and the cooking time is extended. When it is necessary to open the smoker, try to do everything at once: add fuel, add smoking material, and check the water pan. (Keeping the water pan from drying out is vital to maintaining temperature and the proper moist cooking environment.) When you have to open the smoker, also take advantage of the opportunity to spray the pork with the mist mixture. This will keep the surface of the pork moist and provide flavor during the lengthy cooking process.

7. When the meat has started to pull down on the bone about ¼ inch, brush the ribs with the barbecue sauce, and continue to cook until the ribs are fork-tender, about 30 minutes more. The total cooking time will be 3 to 5 hours. Remove the ribs from the smoker, and allow to rest for 10 minutes before slicing into individual ribs.

Silverskin is a thin, tough membrane that covers the full length of ribs on the back, or bone, side (see page 67). Some cooks prefer to leave this membrane on, but most cooks prefer to remove it. Because it is so tough, silverskin can prevent seasoning and smoke from penetrating into the meat.

Slow cooking in an oven can produce decent ribs, but of course they will not have that smoke flavor. If using the oven method, set the temperature at 225° to 250°F.

Jamaican Jerk Chicken

In Jamaica you can purchase jerk chicken or pork from hundreds of roadside stands, where it is often cooked in old oil drums. Jerk is based on two main ingredients: chiles called Scotch Bonnets and what Jamaicans call "pimento," or allspice. The allspice berries from the pimento tree are used in the jerk marinade, and the pimento wood, and sometimes leaves too, are used to smoke the chicken. This is a spicy barbecued dish. If you prefer it very hot, add another Scotch Bonnet chile. If you want it "Jamaican hot," add three chiles. If desired, serve with rice and beans to tame the heat, or simply accompany with a side of your favorite hot sauce and a cold Jamaican beer.

1. Trim the stems off the bottom half of the cilantro bunch and discard; chop the remaining half of the bunch with the leaves.

2. Combine the oil and vinegar in a bowl. Stir in the lime juice, molasses, soy sauce, cilantro, green onions, garlic, chile, bay leaves, thyme, allspice, cinnamon, ginger, black pepper, and nutmeg and mix well to combine.

3. If you cannot purchase chicken halves, purchase whole chickens and ask the butcher at the market to split them. Or, to prepare the halves yourself, cut the chicken down both sides of the backbone. Reserve the backbone for another use. Lay the chicken out on a cutting board skin side down. Cut the breast down one side of the breastbone with a sharp knife. Lay the chicken halves in a baking pan and pour the spice

1 bunch cilantro

⅓ cup olive oil or canola oil

⅓ cup distilled white vinegar

½ cup fresh lime juice

½ cup molasses

¼ cup soy sauce

6 green onions, white and green portions, chopped

2 garlic cloves, chopped

1 Scotch Bonnet chile, seeded and chopped (see Chef's Notes)

3 bay leaves, crushed

1 tbsp dried thyme leaves

(continued)

BARBECUING

mixture on top. Coat the chicken very well with the spice mixture, cover, and refrigerate for 12 hours or up to overnight, turning once.

4. Remove the chicken from the marinade. Reserve the marinade. Allow the chicken to warm slightly at room temperature for 20 minutes before barbecuing.

5. Prepare your smoker or grill, and bring it to a temperature between 225° and 250°F with a light smoke escaping. Place a pan of water below the area where the pork will be cooked; this will keep the meat from drying out, prevent flare-ups, and help maintain the chamber temperature.

6. Cook the chicken at 250°F until it reaches an internal temperature of 165° to 170°F, about 2 hours, basting with the reserved marinade about halfway through the cooking process.

7. Remove the chicken from the smoker or grill and allow to rest for about 15 minutes. In Jamaica, they traditionally whack the chicken into small pieces using a cleaver, which breaks the bones into small pieces. Alternatively, use a large knife to separate the drumstick and thigh from each of the half chickens, then cut the thigh from the breast and cut the breasts crosswise into halves.

1 tbsp freshly ground allspice

1 tsp ground cinnamon

1 tsp ground ginger or 1 tbsp grated fresh ginger

1 tsp freshly ground black pepper

½ tsp ground or freshly grated nutmeg

5 lb chicken halves, bone in

CHEF'S NOTES

Warning! Scotch Bonnet chiles are hot! When handling them, I recommend that you wear gloves. If you're not wearing gloves, be sure to wash your hands immediately after handling the peppers. Be very careful not to touch your eyes, lips, or any other part of your face while you are handling the peppers, or you will get burned. A habañero may be substituted for the Scotch Bonnet.

Pimento is native to Jamaica and some other Caribbean islands. Although true Jerk involves pimento wood, it's getting scarce so it isn't always used even in Jamaica anymore. It does not grow in the United States, but it can be purchased (at great cost) on some Internet sites. You can easily substitute another wood, like apple or cherry.

Smoked Rock Cornish Game Hen with Lentil Ragout

MAKES 6 SERVINGS

These game hens pair perfectly with Lentil Ragout, and like the lentils, the hens can be served hot or cold. Just keep in mind that cold foods impart less flavor, so you may want to add a bit more seasoning if you plan to serve this dish cold. If you decide to serve the game hens with a sauce, such as Classic Barbecue Sauce (page 216) or Creamy Horseradish Sauce (page 223), be sure to keep it on the side, because the birds' skin is not edible (see Chef's Notes).

1. To MAKE THE BRINE: Combine the water, sugar, salt, pickling spice, sage, and thyme in a 2-gallon pot over high heat. Bring to a boil, then reduce the heat and simmer for 10 minutes.

2. Remove the pot from the heat, add enough ice to the pot to bring the water level up to 1 gallon, and allow to cool to below 40°F. Strain the mixture, and chill until ready to use.

3. Remove the wrappers from the game hens, and remove and discard the bags containing the gizzards. Rinse the game hens under cool running water. Place in a plastic container and cover with the brine. Cover the container with a plate to keep the game hens submerged in the brine. Refrigerate for 4 to 6 hours.

4. Remove the game hens from the brine, rinse under cold running water, and transfer to a baking sheet fitted with a roasting rack. Refrigerate for 6 to 12 hours, uncovered. Remove from the refrigerator and allow the game hens to warm slightly at room temperature for 30 minutes before smoking.

BRINE

½ gallon water

½ cup packed dark brown sugar

¼ cup kosher salt

2 tbsp pickling spice

6 sage leaves

12 thyme sprigs

Six 1- to 1½-lb rock Cornish game hens

Lentil Ragout (page 224)

BARBECUING

When you remove the game hens from the smoker, the skin will look beautiful; however, it must be removed. The skin protects the meat during the cooking process, but the smoke and long cooking time make the skin extremely tough and inedible.

This process can be used to cook any type of poultry: A 3- to 4-pound chicken should be brined for 12 hours, may be injected with brine before submerging it in the brine, and will need about 1 gallon of brine; it will take about 5 hours to cook. A 14-pound turkey should be injected with the brine before submerging it in the brine, should be brined for 24 hours, and will need about 5 gallons of brine; it will take about 8 hours to cook.

5. Meanwhile, prepare the smoker or grill for barbecuing: Bring the temperature to 225° to 250°F, fill the water pan, and develop a light smoke. It's important to maintain the proper temperature, so the smoker temperature should stay in the 225° to 250°F range with a small amount of light smoke escaping. Place the game hens into the smoking unit. This will cool the unit off, so it may require some adjustments to get the temperature to settle back in the 225° to 250°F range. You will need a thermometer to constantly monitor the temperature; it's best to have a two-probe remote digital thermometer so that you can put one probe into the chamber and the other into the meat, making sure that the thermometer is not touching any bones.

6. Avoid unnecessarily opening the smoker; it's best to try to go without opening it for an hour or so at a time. Each time you open the cooking unit, heat is lost and the cooking time gets extended. When it is necessary to open the smoker, try to do everything at once: add fuel, add smoking material, and check the water pan. (Keeping the water pan from drying out is vital to maintaining temperature and the proper moist cooking environment.) The game hens are done when they have reached an internal temperature of 165ºF in the thickest part of the thigh, about 3 hours. Remove the game hens from the smoker, loosely cover with aluminum foil, and allow to rest at room temperature for about 20 minutes to allow the juices to redistribute.

7. Remove the skin (see Chef's Notes) and serve immediately, or chill before serving. Serve with the lentil ragout and, if desired, the sauce of your choice on the side.

Smoke-Roasted Duck with Dried Cranberry Sauce

Although this recipe is a nod to traditional roast duck with a sweet-and-sour sauce, it is a unique preparation because the duck is smoke-roasted and served with a sweet-tart sauce made with balsamic vinegar and dried cranberries.

1. TO PREPARE THE DUCK: Remove the duck from the packaging. Remove the package of the liver, heart, and gizzard, and reserve only the gizzards and neck. Remove the tips and middle segment of the wings. Cut the neck and wings into 2-inch pieces and reserve.

2. Rinse the duck under cold running water. Place the duck in the brine, cover, and refrigerate overnight or for up to 24 hours. Remove from the refrigerator and allow the duck to warm slightly, uncovered, at room temperature for 30 minutes before smoking. Take a sharp knife or razor and cut the skin into a diamond pattern about ⅛ inch deep, with 1 inch between each cut; this will allow for more fat to render from the duck while cooking.

3. Meanwhile, prepare your smoker or gas or charcoal grill: Bring the temperature to 225° to 250°F, fill the water pan, and use wood chips or chunks to develop a light smoke. You should see gentle wisps of smoke exiting from the vents. Place the duck into the smoking unit. This will cool the unit off, so it may require some adjustments to get the temperature to settle back in the 225° to 250°F range. If you are having trouble maintaining the minimum temperature, you may need

DUCK

One 4- to 5-lb whole duck

1 gallon basic brine (see chart, page 79), chilled

SAUCE

2 tbsp canola oil

Wings, neck, and gizzard from the duck

7 cups plus 1 tablespoon cold water

2 oranges

1 cup dried cranberries

1 tbsp plus 1 tsp balsamic vinegar

⅔ cup Madeira wine

2 tbsp cornstarch

Kosher salt, as needed

Freshly ground black pepper, as needed

to open the vents wider or add more fuel; if the temperature gets too hot, you can close the vents completely until the temperature drops. You will need a thermometer to constantly monitor the temperature; it's best to have a two-probe remote digital thermometer so that you can put one probe into the chamber and the other into the meat, making sure that the thermometer is not touching any bones.

4. Avoid unnecessarily opening the smoker; it's best to try to go without opening it for an hour or so at a time. Each time you open the cooking unit, heat is lost and the cooking time gets extended. When it is necessary to open the smoker, try to do everything at once: add fuel, add smoking material, and check the water pan. (Keeping the water pan from drying out is vital to maintaining temperature and the proper moist cooking environment.) Cook until the duck reaches an internal temperature of 175°F in the thickest part of the thigh, 4 to 5 hours. (The cooking time can vary widely depending on outside temperature and your control of the chamber temperature.) During this time much of the fat will render from the duck. Unlike smoked chicken, the skin of the duck is edible after smoking due to the high fat content. If you would like the skin to be a little crisper, place the duck into a 500°F oven for 5 to 10 minutes after smoking; this may turn the skin black, but it will not taste bitter. Lightly cover the duck with aluminum foil and allow it to rest for about 20 minutes before carving.

5. WHILE THE DUCK IS COOKING, PREPARE THE SAUCE: Heat the oil in a 2-quart sauce pot over medium-high heat. Add the reserved duck pieces and cook until browned, about 5 minutes. Add 5 cups of the cold water and bring to a very gentle simmer. Simmer until the broth has reduced to 1 cup. Strain the broth, discard the solids, and skim off any excess fat from the broth.

6. While the broth is simmering, using a sharp knife or zester, cut long, thin strips of zest from the oranges. (Use only the orange-colored portion of the peel; avoid the white, pithy portion, which is very bitter.) Bring 2 cups of the water to a boil over high heat, add the orange zest, and simmer until the zest is tender, about 5 minutes. Strain, rinse, dry, and reserve the zest.

7. Squeeze the juice from the oranges into a bowl, add the cranberries, and set aside to soak for at least 30 minutes.

8. Combine the broth, vinegar, and cranberries in juice in a sauce pot. Bring to a gentle simmer over medium-high heat. Simmer until the mixture has reduced by half. Add the orange zest and Madeira, and bring the mixture back to a simmer.

9. Combine the cornstarch with the remaining 1 tablespoon of water and mix until smooth. While whisking the simmering sauce, add the cornstarch mixture in a slow, steady stream. Increase the heat to bring the sauce to a boil, then remove it from the heat. Season with salt and pepper.

10. To carve the duck: Starting at the breastbone, cut the skin on one side down to the bone. Keep cutting down the side of the duck to remove the breast. Do the same on the other side to remove the other breast. Cut the legs and thighs from the carcass. Trim any excess fat or skin from the breasts and legs. Serve with the sauce.

If desired, accompany with Garlic Whipped Potatoes (page 173), Lentil Ragout (page 224), Spoonbread (page 205), or Soft Polenta (page 203). If preparing the Soft Polenta, replace the Parmesan with raclette or Swiss cheese to better complement the duck.

BARBECUING

Maple-Glazed Grilled Salmon

Being from New Hampshire, I have a fondness for maple syrup. Maple and smoke are a very natural combination. The balance of the smoke, the sweetness of the maple, and the saltiness of the soy sauce makes for a delicious and unusual dish. You could also try using maple wood chips to provide the smoke and experiment with other types of fish.

1. Combine the maple syrup, lemon juice, soy sauce, sesame oil, and garlic to make a marinade.

2. Layer the 6 salmon fillets, skin side down, in a 1-gallon zip-close plastic bag. Pour half of the marinade into the bag with the salmon. Reserve the remaining marinade. Squeeze out any excess air from the plastic bag and seal it tightly. Place the bag in the refrigerator and allow the salmon to marinate for 3 to 4 hours, turning the bag over occasionally.

3. Meanwhile, prepare a gas or charcoal grill or smoker for smoking. The temperature of the chamber should be 180° to 200°F with a steady stream of light smoke exiting the vents. Place a pan of ice in the chamber, if needed, to keep the temperature low and give the salmon more exposure to the smoke; you can also freeze water in the smoker's water pan.

½ cup maple syrup

½ cup fresh lemon juice

¼ cup soy sauce

1 tsp sesame oil

2 tsp minced garlic

6 salmon fillets, skin on (about 6 oz each)

2 tbsp vegetable oil

Remove the salmon from the bag and discard the marinade. Pat the skin side dry with paper towels and brush it lightly with the vegetable oil. Place the salmon into the chamber of the grill or smoker, skin side down. Cook the salmon until the thickest part of the flesh reaches an internal temperature of 145°F, about 1 hour. You can use a thermometer or you can use a paring knife to make a small cut and take a peek to check that the center of the salmon fillet is cooked; it should be light pink in color.

4. Serve the reserved unused marinade with the salmon as a dipping sauce.

Hot Smoked Salmon

This is a very versatile recipe that makes for tasty leftovers, so it is advised for you to make extra. Unlike the cold smoked salmon used for lox on bagels with cream cheese, which has a sliceable, almost raw texture, this is a hot smoked fish that will have a firmer, flakier, more cooked texture.

One 2- to 2½-lb salmon fillet, skin on

CURE

1 cup kosher salt

½ cup sugar

1 tsp garlic powder

1 tsp onion powder

1 tsp freshly cracked white or black pepper

1 tbsp grated lemon zest

1. Place the salmon on a baking sheet with the skin side down. Using the backside of a knife, lightly scrape the flesh to remove any scales. Remove any pin bones that run down the center of the fillet: Rub your finger against the grain, from head to tail, to feel for these tiny pin bones. They run about two-thirds of the way down the fish. When you feel them, pull them out using tweezers or fish pliers.

2. TO MAKE THE CURE: Combine the salt, sugar, garlic powder, onion powder, pepper, and lemon zest. Sprinkle the cure liberally over the salmon. Use all of the cure mixture, covering thicker portions of the fish with more of the cure. Refrigerate for 2 hours.

3. Rinse the salmon under cool running water and place on a wire rack. Carefully pat the fish dry with paper towels. You will notice that the salmon is now a bright red color and is much firmer. Refrigerate for 12 hours, uncovered, to allow the fish to dry thoroughly. When the salmon is removed from the refrigerator, it should feel dry and tacky to the touch. The salmon must be dry; if it isn't, the smoke will not stick.

4. Meanwhile, prepare your smoker or gas or charcoal grill. The chamber temperature should be between 180° and 200°F with a steady stream of light smoke exiting from the vents. Place a pan of ice in the smoker if needed to keep the temperature low and to give the salmon more exposure to the smoke; you can also freeze water in the smoker's water pan while the salmon is drying. Place the salmon onto the chamber rack in the smoking unit. Cook the salmon until the exterior of the flesh is a golden color, the center is still pink but not raw and fleshy, and the thickest part of the flesh has reached an internal temperature of 145°F, about 2 hours or less. You can use a thermometer or make a small cut with a paring knife and take a peek inside the flesh to check for doneness. You do not want to see white pools of juice that have escaped from the fish and coagulated on top; that is a sign that the fish is overcooked.

5. Remove the salmon from the smoker and allow it to cool slightly. When it has cooled, the surface of the fish should be covered with a dry, reflective glaze; this is called a pellicle and is desirable in smoked fish. Peel off the skin and cut the salmon into equal portions.

It is very common, although not critical, to use alder wood for smoking fish, because alder naturally imparts sweet overtones during the smoking process.

You can substitute any other fish fillets in this recipe. The cooking time will vary depending on the type of fish.

There is no limit to the ways you can serve this dish. Serve as an entrée with asparagus and Carolina Mustard Sauce (page 219), as pictured; use it to top Boston lettuce with Lemon Vinaigrette (page 209); serve as an hors d'oeuvre with Sauce Lamaze (page 226) or Creamy Horseradish Sauce (page 223); use as a filling for quiche; or serve as a spread or dip for Melba toast, crackers, apple slices, and so on (see Smoked Salmon Spread on page 208).

Smoked Trout with Apple-Horseradish Cream

MAKES 6 APPETIZER SERVINGS

This is great way for trout fishermen to prepare their catch. Even if you don't catch your own fish, this is an economical way to have smoked trout. Smoke and horseradish are a classic flavor combination; the apple adds sweetness that helps balance the flavor of the smoked fish. This recipe is for an appetizer portion. If you'd like to serve it as an entrée, you can simply double all of the ingredient quantities and serve it with a vegetable side dish, such as asparagus or green beans. As an entrée, it's attractive served family-style on a large platter.

1. Lay the trout fillets skin side down on a baking sheet. Using the backside of a knife, lightly scrape the flesh to remove any scales. Using tweezers, remove any bones.

2. Combine the salt, sugar, garlic powder, onion powder, pepper, and lemon zest. Sprinkle the mixture liberally over the trout fillets, covering the thin belly and tail sections with a ¹⁄₁₆-inch layer and the thicker sections of the trout with a ¼-inch layer of the salt mixture. Refrigerate for 30 minutes.

3. Rinse the trout under cool running water and place on a wire rack. Pat dry with paper towels. You will notice that the trout feels much firmer. Refrigerate, uncovered, for 6 to 12 hours to allow the trout to dry. When it is removed from the refrigerator, the trout should feel very dry and may be tacky to the touch. The trout must be dry or the smoke will not stick.

4. Meanwhile, prepare your smoker or gas or charcoal grill. The chamber temperature should be 160° to 200°F with a steady stream of light smoke exiting

6 boneless trout fillets (about 3 oz each), skin on

1 cup kosher salt

½ cup sugar

1 tbsp garlic powder

1 tsp onion powder

1 tsp freshly cracked black pepper

Grated zest of 2 lemons

2 cups mixed greens (preferably baby lettuces)

1 cup Lemon Vinaigrette (page 209)

1 cup Apple-Horseradish Cream (page 222)

18 to 24 unpeeled green apple slices

BARBECUING

131

from the vents. Place a pan of ice inside the smoker; you can also freeze ice in the smoker's water pan. The ice will help to maintain the low temperature and ensure that the trout has more exposure to the smoke. Place the trout fillets onto racks and place in the smoking unit. Smoke until the trout is a golden color and cooked through, about 1 hour or less. You can use a paring knife to make a small cut to take a peek at the center of the trout to check the doneness. You do not want to see white pools of juice that have escaped from the fish and coagulated on top, because that is a sign the fish is overcooked.

5. Remove the trout from the smoker and allow to cool. The surface of the fish should have a dry, reflective glaze on it. This is called the pellicle and is desirable in smoked fish. Peel off the skin and refrigerate the trout until ready to serve.

6. Toss the greens with the vinaigrette.

7. Divide the greens among 6 plates. Place a rounded tablespoon of the Apple-Horseradish Cream on each plate beside the greens (or pipe it using a pastry bag fitted with a star tip for a more decorative presentation). Top each serving of greens with a trout fillet, and garnish each plate with 3 or 4 apple slices.

Smoked Shrimp with Sauce Lamaze

This is not one of those traditional shrimp cocktails where the cocktail sauce totally dominates the fish flavor. The shrimp in this appetizer have a beautiful golden color, and the Sauce Lamaze is a subtle complement to the smoky shrimp flavor.

1. TO MAKE THE MARINADE: Combine the wine, oil, orange zest, sage, if using, the garlic, pepper, salt, and rosemary in a large bowl. Add the shrimp, cover the bowl, and place in the refrigerator for 2 to 3 hours to marinate.

2. Drain the shrimp and discard the marinade. Pat the shrimp dry with paper towels. Slide 4 shrimp onto 2 skewers placed side by side—the extra skewer will allow you to more easily manage the shrimp and turn them more quickly when they're being smoked. Repeat, using 2 skewers for every 4 shrimp, to create 6 portions. If using bamboo skewers, soak them in water for about 10 minutes first to lower the possibility of burning. Very lightly brush the shrimp with the vegetable oil.

3. About 1 hour before you plan to start cooking, prepare your smoker or gas or charcoal grill. The chamber temperature should be 160° to 200°F with a steady stream of smoke exiting from the vents. Place a pan of ice inside the smoker; you can also freeze ice in the smoker's water pan ahead of time. This is not a critical step but it will help maintain a low temperature in the chamber and help the shrimp have more

MARINADE

1 cup dry white wine

⅓ cup olive oil

2 tbsp grated orange zest

2 tbsp minced sage (optional)

2 garlic cloves, crushed

1 tbsp freshly cracked black pepper

1½ tsp kosher salt

1 tsp rosemary leaves

24 medium or large shrimp (22/25 or 16/20 count), peeled and deveined

¼ cup vegetable oil

Sauce Lamaze (page 226), as needed

exposure to the smoke. Place the skewered shrimp onto racks and place inside the smoking unit. Cook the shrimp until they are a golden smoky color, about 1 hour, turning the shrimp over about halfway through the cooking process. You can use a paring knife to cut into one of the shrimp to check for doneness if you are not sure. Remove the shrimp from the smoker and chill in the refrigerator.

4. Serve chilled, with the sauce on the side.

4 SLOW ROASTING

Roasting is a dry heat cooking method where the item is either cooked near an open flame, such as on a spit over a grill, or more commonly in an oven. While the meat is roasting, the surface is browning, crisping, and being basted with its own fat or an added fat. Roasting is usually performed on tender, less active, larger, multiple portion-sized muscles. For example, most people associate roasting with a golden brown roast chicken or a Thanksgiving turkey. Slow roasting applies the same dry heat to cook flavorful, less tender cuts of meat such as pork shoulder, lamb shanks, or beef ribs but at a much lower temperature—between 200° and 250°F—over a longer period of time.

LIKE ROASTING, SLOW ROASTING employs the indirect heat of an oven to cook the food. The heat is conducted to the meat by the hot surrounding air. It browns and crisps the exterior and penetrates into the meat, warms the juices, and turns them into steam, which cooks the interior. The resulting juices that are forced out of the meat are called fond, or pan drippings. They are collected in the roasting pan and used to prepare the sauce to accompany the roast. Slow roasting may require an extended period of time to cook, but it generally does not require a lot of attention while cooking. As a reward for your patience, your house will be filled with an incredible aroma that stimulates your appetite. The meat will be very flavorful, tender, and juicy, with a crispy exterior, and the accompanying sauce will add even more texture and flavor to the dish. Less tender, and typically less expensive, cuts of meat are usually used. The finished meat and sauce hold well and are sometimes even better the next day, and leftovers are very versatile, meaning that you will often get several different meals from one product.

Slow roasting utilizes large, less tender, less expensive, more active, higher-fat muscles that contain a large amount of connective tissue called "collagen." These cuts contain two types of fat: intramuscular fat, which refers to the strips of fat streaked within the muscle, also known as marbling; and chunks of fat within the cut or found externally on the meat. For example, a pork butt contains as much as 33 percent fat, which makes it perfect for this cooking technique. As the meat cooks, the collagen dissolves into gelatin, which makes the meat tender and juicy, and the fat melts and bastes the meat, adding flavor and moisture. The finished meat will have a smooth texture and mouthfeel and a succulent quality. Another advantage of using more active and less tender types of meat is that they produce finished dishes with deep, full flavor and rich texture. You can, however, also slow roast tender cuts of meat. Cuts like sirloin roast or prime rib roast benefit from slow roasting because they experience less shrinkage, which equates to a higher yield and a moister final product. Slow-roasted meat will also be more evenly cooked. These items are pulled from the oven at a much lower internal temperature than less tender cuts of meat, usually 125° to 130°F for medium rare.

Preparing and Cooking the Meat

TRIM THE MEAT of most of its external fat before slow roasting. If the item has a thick layer of fat on top, such as a pork butt, trim it down to a ¼- or ½-inch-thick layer. Then season the meat. Seasoning can vary from simply using salt and pepper to slathering the meat with prepared mustard to using a twelve-ingredient dry rub. The item can be cooked right away or refrigerated for hours or overnight to allow the seasonings to penetrate the meat.

The meat should be removed from the refrigerator 30 minutes before roasting and allowed to sit at room temperature while the oven is preheating. This allows the meat to warm slightly so it will cook more evenly and not lower the oven temperature as much when you place it in the oven. A general rule of thumb to determine cooking time would be to calculate up to 1½ hours for each pound of meat. An 8-pound pork butt, for example, can take 10 to 12 hours to cook. If you are under a meal deadline, it is advisable to start the roast 2 hours earlier than the estimated cooking time to give you a cushion. Slow-roasted meat holds well and can be reheated, if

necessary, so it is better to finish cooking it earlier than to be caught waiting for it to finish cooking because it could be a long wait.

Even with a low-and-slow cooking method, the meat can be overcooked, so it's important to catch the meat at the correct time. When the meat is cooked too long, it will render too much of its juices, gelatin, and fat, which will make the meat dry, tough, and stringy. There are several ways to determine doneness. You can pull at the meat; if it separates easily and is tender and juicy, it is done. It can be stabbed with a long wooden skewer or fork; if the fork removes easily and the meat does not hang onto it, the meat is cooked. However, the best and most accurate way is to use a thermometer. An instant-read probe thermometer can be inserted into the meat periodically to check the temperature for doneness. An even better way is to use a probe that is connected by a thin wire to a digital thermometer outside the oven that continually monitors the process of roasting the meat. Many ovens today have these built in. If you are looking for the product to be sliceable, then pull the meat from the oven when it reaches 185°F. If you are looking for a product that will be "pulled" or chopped, then cook it to an internal temperature of 192°F. Allow the meat to rest for about 20 minutes to let the juices inside redistribute before being cut or pulled, otherwise those hard-earned juices will flow out of the meat onto the cutting board and the meat will be dry.

Preparing the Sauce

WHILE THE MEAT IS RESTING, a sauce can be prepared from the collection of intensely flavorful meat drippings that form at the bottom of the roasting pan. (The roast and the rack need to be removed from the roasting pan before the sauce can be made.)

There are several ways to prepare a sauce from the pan drippings. The simplest is to prepare a jus. Drain the excess fat from the pan and place the pan over low to medium heat. Add water or stock to the pan, scrape up the drippings with a wooden spoon, and allow them to dissolve into the liquid. At this point the liquid should be tasted and seasoned and then strained to remove any solids. This thin juice, or jus, is intensely flavored and served with the meat as is. A jus lié is prepared by thickening the jus lightly with some arrowroot or cornstarch.

Another common and popular way to prepare a sauce from the drippings is to make a pan gravy. If any juices, aside from fat, remain in the pan, place the pan over medium-high heat and bring the juices to a simmer. Before the drippings start to burn, drain most of the fat and discard it. Leave enough fat in the pan to absorb the flour later in the process. Vegetables can be added to the pan and browned to provide more flavor and color. Whisk some flour into the fat and cook for several minutes. At this point, add some cold stock to the pan, whisk it into the flour mixture, and bring it to a simmer. It must be simmered for at least 25 minutes to cook out the starchy flour taste. While simmering, add more stock if the sauce gets too thick, or continue to simmer to reduce the sauce if it is too thin. Once it reaches the desired consistency, the pan gravy can be seasoned, strained, and served with the meat.

SLOW ROASTING: STEP BY STEP

1.

Place the roasting pan in the oven, and monitor the temperature of the meat with a thermometer.

2.

Near the end of the cooking time, add any desired vegetables to be roasted to the pan underneath the meat and rack.

3.

When it is done, the meat should be fork-tender and separate easily, with a rich texture and full flavor.

4.

Make a pan sauce or gravy from the drippings that collect in the pan. If desired, strain the pan gravy before serving.

5.

Use a kitchen fork to steady the roast while you carve the meat with a large slicing knife.

Oven-Roasted Pork Butt with Pan Gravy,
Whipped Potatoes (page 173), and Roasted Root Vegetables (page 170)

Oven-Roasted Pork Butt with Pan Gravy

MAKES 6 SERVINGS

One 6- to 8-lb pork butt, bone in

BRINE

1 cup water

½ tsp kosher salt

½ tsp packed brown sugar

RUB

2 tbsp kosher salt

1 tbsp sugar

2 tsp freshly cracked black pepper

1 tsp caraway seeds (see Chef's Note)

Grated zest of 1 lemon

PAN GRAVY

1 cup chopped onion

½ cup chopped carrot

½ cup red wine

¼ cup tomato paste

½ cup all-purpose flour

1 qt chicken or pork broth, chilled, plus more as needed

Kosher salt, as needed

Freshly ground black pepper, as needed

1. If the skin is still on the pork, remove it along with most of the exterior fat, leaving no more than a ¼-inch-thick layer.

2. TO MAKE THE BRINE: Combine the water, salt, and sugar and stir until dissolved. When the ingredients have dissolved, draw the brine into a brining needle. Using the needle, puncture the meat all the way to its center, and inject the brine evenly into the pork while slowly extracting the needle from the meat at the same time. Make multiple insertions into the meat until all of the brine has been injected. If you do not have a brining needle, this step can be omitted.

3. TO MAKE THE RUB: Combine the salt, sugar, pepper, caraway seeds, and lemon zest. Massage the rub into the pork and wrap the pork tightly in plastic wrap. Place the wrapped pork into a large brining bag and store in the refrigerator for 12 to 24 hours.

4. Remove the pork from the refrigerator. Unwrap it, but do not rinse it. Place it fat side up in a roasting pan fitted with a rack. Preheat the oven to 250°F and let the pork rest at room temperature for 30 minutes while the oven is preheating.

5. Insert a probe into the center of the pork, avoiding any bones or fat pockets. (A fat pocket can be easily seen; it is between the seams of muscles on the side of the butt that does not contain the bone.) Attach

143

the other end of the probe into a thermometer so that you can monitor the internal temperature of the pork while it is cooking. (This option may also be available on your oven.)

6. Place the pork on the center shelf of the oven. Roast with the fat side up for 2 hours. Turn the pork over and roast it with the fat side down for 2 more hours. Turn the pork over a final time and allow it to finish roasting with the fat side up. Each time you turn the pork, check to make sure that the juices have not dried up and are not burning on the bottom of the roasting pan. If the pan is dry, add a few tablespoons of water. The pan drippings are important to the sauce preparation and should not be allowed to burn.

7. The pork's temperature will stay around 160°F for an extended period of time, as long as 2 hours. You may start to doubt your thermometer, but it is not broken (see page 70). Be patient. When the temperature breaks away from this plateau, and moves above 170°F, add the onion and carrot to the pan. At this point, begin to watch the meat more closely, because the temperature will now increase steadily. When the pork has reached an internal temperature of 185°F, remove it from the oven. Cooking to this temperature will leave enough texture in the meat for it to be easily sliced; if you would like to serve the meat pulled, in large chunks, or chopped, allow the pork to reach an internal temperature of 193°F before removing it from the oven. Allow the pork to rest, loosely covered with aluminum foil.

8. WHILE THE PORK IS RESTING, PREPARE THE PAN GRAVY: Remove the pork and rack from the roasting pan. Drain off and discard all but 2 tablespoons of the fat, being careful not to pour out any of the pan drippings or vegetables.

9. Place the roasting pan on the stovetop over medium heat and add ¼ cup of the red wine to help lift and dissolve the juices and particles that have accumulated in the bottom of the roasting pan during cooking. It's important that these juices and

particles on the bottom of the pan are not burnt, since they provide the majority of the sauce's flavor. Simmer until all the wine has evaporated and only the fat is remaining. Add the tomato paste and cook, stirring constantly, until the tomato paste has lost its red color and caramelized to a deep brown. Add the remaining ¼ cup red wine and cook until all the wine has evaporated. When the wine has evaporated, add the flour and continue to cook, stirring constantly, for 2 minutes. Whisk in the broth until everything is dissolved in the broth. Increase the heat to bring the mixture to a boil, then reduce the heat to establish a gentle simmer. Simmer until the gravy reaches the desired consistency, at least 25 minutes. While the gravy is simmering, taste it periodically and season it with salt and pepper if necessary. If the gravy is too thin, continue reducing it until it thickens to the proper consistency; if it is too thick, thin it as needed with more broth. Adjust the seasoning with additional salt and pepper, if necessary, and then strain the gravy into a bowl or serving dish to remove any lumps.

10. Remove the bones from the pork, slice, pull, or chop the meat, and serve with the pan gravy.

SLOW ROASTING

Lechón (Puerto Rican–Style Roast Suckling Pig)

One of the most memorable food experiences I've ever had is eating lechón from a panel truck on the side of a road in Puerto Rico. It was delicious and still stands out in my mind as one of the best foods I've ever tasted. In Puerto Rico this dish would be served with Ajili-Mojili (page 231), a hot pepper and garlic sauce. If you just can't get past the thought of cooking a whole pig, substitute a whole pork shoulder, scale down the marinade accordingly, and follow the same method.

1. Grind the cumin seeds, black pepper, coriander seeds, and bay leaves into a powder using a mortar and pestle or food processor. Add the garlic, oregano, salt, and cayenne and grind or pulse until incorporated. Add the naranja agria and olive oil to form a smooth, loose paste.

2. Rub the entire pig with the paste. Place the pig in a large plastic bag, such as a garbage bag, squeeze out as much of the excess air as possible, and refrigerate overnight. Remove the pig from the refrigerator 1 hour before cooking, and allow it to sit at room temperature in order to remove some of the chill.

3. If spit roasting, set up your spit roaster with low, indirect heat. A water pan will need to be placed under the pig to prevent a fire. If using the grill method (the traditional method of doing lechón), bank the hot coals on two sides of the pig. Place a water pan under the pig to prevent flare-ups. Cover and maintain a temperature of 300°F. If using the oven method, place the pig onto a roasting rack fitted

3 tbsp cumin seeds

2 tbsp freshly cracked black pepper

1 tbsp coriander seeds

2 bay leaves, crushed

15 large garlic heads, peeled, cloves chopped

3 tbsp chopped oregano

⅓ cup kosher salt

1 tsp cayenne pepper

1 cup naranja agria (sour orange juice; see Chef's Notes)

½ cup olive oil

One 15- to 18-lb dressed suckling pig, kidneys removed (see Chef's Notes)

over an aluminum foil–lined baking sheet. If using a convection oven, set the temperature at 275°F. For a conventional oven, set the temperature at 300°F.

4. Cook the pig until it reaches an internal temperature of 160°F in the leg and shoulder areas. (The cooking time will depend entirely on the size of the pig. A 15- to 18-pound pig will take 5 to 6 hours to cook and will turn a deep mahogany color.) Be careful when removing the pig from the oven; there will be a fair amount of hot fat on the baking sheet. To avoid spills, it is advisable to drain the fat about halfway through the cooking process.

5. Allow the pig to rest for 30 minutes before carving. Remove the skin and serve each person a mixture of meat from the leg, shoulder, and loin areas along with some of the crunchy skin.

You can find naranja agria at Latin food stores and some supermarkets and online. If it is unavailable, substitute a mixture of 1 cup fresh orange juice, 1½ teaspoons fresh lemon juice, and 1½ teaspoons fresh lime juice.

If you are planning to use the oven method, keep in mind that it may be a challenge to fit a pig larger than 18 pounds into a home oven. You will probably have to special order the pig from a meat purveyor or butcher.

SLOW ROASTING

Slow-Roasted Pork Belly with Asian-Style Dipping Sauce (page 221) and Brussels Sprout Slaw (page 165)

Slow-Roasted Pork Belly

MAKES 6 SERVINGS

This fatty slab of pork is the same part of the pig that bacon comes from, but it is not smoked or sliced like bacon. Slow roasting renders some of the fat out of the pork belly, crisps the skin, and makes the meat deliciously tender.

1. Preheat the oven to 275°F.

2. Cut the onions in half through the middle and place the halves, cut side down, in a roasting pan large enough to accommodate the pork belly.

3. Using a sharp knife, pierce the skin of the pork belly and score it at 1-inch intervals along the full length of the belly; this will allow more fat to render from the pork during roasting. Rub the olive oil into the pork belly. Sprinkle with the salt and pepper and rub them into the meat.

4. Add the thyme and 1 cup of the chicken broth to the roasting pan. Place the pork, skin side up, into the pan on top the onion halves. Transfer to the oven and roast until the pork reaches an internal temperature of 193°F, up to 4 hours. Keep periodically checking the pan during cooking to make sure it does not get dry; if it does start to go dry at any point, add more chicken broth. If you have used all of the chicken broth, just add water. It is important not to let the pan dry out, because the pan drippings will fry up in the rendered fat and make the sauce taste bitter.

2 yellow onions, peeled

2½ lb pork belly, skin on

2 tbsp olive oil

1 tbsp kosher salt, plus more as needed

½ tsp freshly cracked black pepper, plus more as needed

10 sprigs thyme

1 to 2 cups chicken broth

½ cup white wine

5. Remove the pork from the pan, and allow it to rest for 20 minutes.

6. While the pork is resting, drain all of the pork fat from the pan, leaving the pan drippings. Add the wine to the drippings in the pan and bring to a simmer on the stovetop over medium heat, scraping up any brown bits that have stuck to the bottom of the pan. Continue simmering until the raw wine flavor has mellowed, about 10 minutes, adding more chicken broth or water, as necessary, to keep the pan from drying out.

7. Strain the sauce into a bowl and discard the onions and herbs.

8. Cut the crispy skin, or "crackling," off of the pork belly and break it into pieces.

9. Slice the pork into 6 portions. Serve each portion with about 2 tablespoons of the sauce and top with the cracklings.

Slow-Roasted Lamb Shoulder

MAKES 6 SERVINGS

Lamb shoulder is a very delicious and economical cut of lamb. Like pork shoulder or pork butt, it is less tender and higher in fat, which makes it an ideal cut for slow roasting or barbecuing. During the cooking process much of the fat will be rendered, making the meat very tender and succulent. It's always best to use domestic lamb (because you just can't beat the quality of lamb from the U.S.A.), but if you can't find it I recommend choosing Australian lamb before New Zealand lamb. This preparation is also a one-pot meal, which makes for easy cleanup.

1. Place a pan of warm water on the lowest shelf of the oven, and preheat the oven to 275°F.

2. Combine 1 tablespoon of the olive oil, the minced garlic, 1½ teaspoons of the salt, and ½ teaspoon of the pepper.

3. Trim the lamb shoulder of excess fat. Rub the garlic mixture onto the lamb, massaging it into the meat. Place the lamb in a roasting pan fitted with a rack, and add the rosemary and thyme to the pan.

4. Transfer the uncovered pan to the oven, on the shelf above the water pan. Roast for 5 hours, basting the lamb occasionally with the fat and juices that accumulate in the pan. Refill the water pan as needed so that it doesn't go dry during roasting.

5. Meanwhile, combine the potatoes, onions, carrots, turnip, and garlic cloves with the remaining 2 tablespoons olive oil, 1½ teaspoons salt, and ½ teaspoon pepper. After the lamb has roasted for 5 hours, add the vegetables to the pan and continue roasting.

3 tbsp extra-virgin olive oil

1 tbsp finely minced garlic, plus 18 whole garlic cloves, peels on

1 tbsp kosher salt

1 tsp freshly cracked black pepper

One 6-lb lamb shoulder, square cut, bone in

½ bunch rosemary, cut into 2-inch pieces

6 sprigs thyme

1 lb unpeeled yellow creamer or new potatoes (about 12)

18 small white boiling onions

½ lb carrots, peeled and cut into 1-inch lengths

(continued)

SLOW ROASTING

6. Roast the lamb until it reaches an internal temperature of 190°F, 6 to 8 hours. Like a pork butt or shoulder, it will plateau in the 165° to 175°F range for 1 to 2 hours as the fat renders out of the meat (see page 70). Be patient, the meat will quickly go up to 190°F as soon as enough fat has rendered. If any of the vegetables are done before the lamb has finished cooking, remove them from the pan and reserve. If any of the vegetables are not done when the lamb is finished, remove the lamb and continue to roast the vegetables. When the lamb and all the vegetables are done, remove them from the pan, and allow the lamb to rest. Drain the fat out of the roasting pan and reserve.

7. To make a pan gravy: Place the roasting pan on the stovetop over medium heat. Add the red wine to deglaze the pan, using a wooden spoon to scrape the bottom of the pan and loosen the drippings. Continue cooking until the wine has reduced by half. Transfer the wine mixture to a 1-quart saucepan. Add the broth, and bring the mixture to a simmer over medium-high heat.

2 cups peeled and diced yellow turnip

1 cup red wine

2 cups lamb, chicken, or vegetable broth

3 tbsp all-purpose flour

1 cup roughly chopped mint leaves

8. Meanwhile, heat 2 tablespoons of the reserved lamb fat in a separate pan over medium heat. Add the flour and cook, stirring constantly, for 3 minutes. Add the flour mixture to the simmering broth, stirring constantly. Simmer for 18 minutes. Stir in the mint and simmer gently for 2 minutes more. If the pan gravy is too thin at this point, simmer longer to reduce it to the proper consistency. If the gravy is too thick, thin it with more broth or water. Strain the pan gravy into a bowl or serving dish and serve with the lamb and vegetables.

This lamb can't be carved like other roasts because the bones get in the way. Simply pull and cut the meat away from the bone and serve it in pieces.

This is a hearty fall or winter dish, but it can be lightened up by replacing the pan gravy with Chimichurri Sauce (page 228). If you decide not to make the pan gravy, be sure to deglaze the pan and freeze the pan drippings for later use.

SLOW ROASTING

Spit-Roasted Garlic and Lime Chicken

This recipe is very easy to prepare and bursting with flavor. If you do not have a rotisserie, you can roast the chicken in the oven in a roasting pan fitted with a roasting rack.

1. TO MAKE THE MARINADE: Combine the lime zest and juice, olive oil, sesame oil, garlic, salt, and pepper in a bowl. Reserve.

2. Rinse the chicken under cool running water. Fill the cavity with 4 of the reserved lime rinds. Truss the chicken, place it into a 1-gallon zip-close plastic bag, and cover it with the marinade. Remove as much air as possible from the bag and seal it tightly. Refrigerate for at least 2 hours or overnight, turning the chicken occasionally while it marinates. Refrigerate overnight for the best flavor.

3. Set up your grill's rotisserie according to the manufacturer's instructions. To avoid flare-ups, place a water pan under the rotisserie. If using the oven, preheat the oven to 375°F.

4. Remove the chicken from the bag and reserve the marinade in a 1-quart pot. Secure the chicken on the spit and transfer it to the rotisserie, or place it in a roasting pan fitted with a roasting rack and transfer to the oven.

MARINADE

1 tsp grated lime zest, plus ¾ cup freshly squeezed lime juice (about 5 limes), rinds reserved (see Chef's Note)

1 tsp extra-virgin olive oil

1 tsp sesame oil

2 tbsp chopped garlic (see Chef's Note)

1 tsp kosher salt

½ tsp freshly cracked black pepper

One 3- to 4-lb whole chicken

OPPOSITE: Spit-Roasted Garlic and Lime Chicken with Roasted Red Pepper and Olive Salad (page 194)

5. Bring the marinade to a boil over high heat. Remove from the heat and use it to periodically baste the chicken.

6. The chicken is done when it reaches an internal temperature of 165°F in the thickest part of the thigh. Remove the chicken from the spit or oven and allow it to rest for 20 minutes before serving.

Fresh garlic and freshly squeezed lime juice are critical to the flavor of this recipe; you cannot substitute bottled lime juice or squeeze the juice a day ahead.

Slow-Roasted Duck Legs

MAKES 6 SERVINGS

This dish is quite similar to duck confit but without the hassle of dealing with all the fat. The cooking time is shorter and the cure is lighter, but the flavor and texture is comparable so in many instances they can be used interchangeably.

1. Rinse the duck legs under cold running water and pat dry with paper towels. Do not trim off any fat.

2. Combine the salt, pepper, thyme, and bay leaf. Sprinkle the mixture on the duck legs and place them into a pan or baking dish. Cover with plastic wrap and set another pan on top. Place a heavy object, such as a large can of vegetables or a foil-wrapped brick, on top to press the legs. Refrigerate overnight or up to 24 hours.

3. Preheat the oven to 275°F. Remove the duck legs from the pan, rinse under cool running water, and pat dry with paper towels. Arrange the legs in a single layer, skin side down, in a large ovenproof pan or cast-iron skillet. It is important not to overcrowd the pan; if necessary, use two pans to cook the legs. Transfer the pan to the oven. Check the duck legs about 30 minutes into the cooking process. If there is ¼ inch of fat or more in the pan, turn the legs over, so that the skin side is up, cover the pan with aluminum foil, and return it to the oven. Continue roasting until the legs have reached an internal temperature of 190°F and are tender, 1 to 2 hours depending on the size of the duck legs. To check for doneness, stick a wooden

6 duck legs (3 to 4 lb total), bone in, thighs and drumstick attached

1½ tsp kosher salt

1 tsp freshly cracked black pepper

4 sprigs thyme or ½ tsp dried thyme

1 bay leaf, crumbled

skewer into the meat; the meat should not hang on the skewer when it is removed. The duck legs will have a bland appearance and should not look caramelized. Reserve the duck fat.

4. To serve, heat 2 to 3 tablespoons of the reserved duck fat in a pan on the stovetop over medium-high heat until it reaches its smoke point, the point at which very light wisps of smoke from the fat start at the edge of the pan. Sear the duck legs in the fat on both sides until caramelized and crisped, about 5 minutes. Duck legs are very versatile and match well with a variety of foods.

The legs can be roasted the day ahead, refrigerated, and seared and warmed in some of the reserved duck fat before serving. To reserve the duck legs for later use, separate the duck legs from the fat after removing the pan from the oven. Allow both to cool at room temperature for about 30 minutes. Place the legs into a storage container, cover, and reserve in the refrigerator for up to a week. Reserve and refrigerate the fat to reheat the duck legs. When ready to serve, sear them as described at left.

Serve about 12 ounces of bone-in duck per plate as an entrée, or serve in any way that you would use duck confit. Pair with Oven-Roasted Potatoes (page 172), Lentil Ragout (page 224), Roasted Root Vegetables (page 170), fresh figs, or pull the meat from the bone and serve on a green salad with Almond-Fig Vinaigrette (page 211).

After preparing the duck legs, be sure to reserve any excess fat. It is great to use for sautéing potatoes or other vegetables.

Duck Confit

The traditional confit cooking method for duck is a method of preservation. The duck is cured, cooked very slowly in its own fat, and then stored, covered with that fat. It can be stored in the refrigerator for 4 months, so prepare more than you need. Keeping duck confit on hand in your refrigerator makes for a quick and easy meal. It can be served warm with crisped skin as described in this recipe, served warm or cold as a salad with greens or lentils, or used as an ingredient in another recipe, such a cassoulet.

1. Combine the salt, pepper, thyme, and bay leaves.

2. Rinse the duck legs under cold running water and pat dry with paper towels. Rub the duck with the salt mixture and place in a glass or ceramic baking dish. Cover the duck with plastic wrap and set a plate or pan on top. Place a heavy object, such as a large can of vegetables or a foil-wrapped brick, on top to press the duck while it is curing. Cure for 36 to 48 hours in the refrigerator.

3. Preheat the oven to 190°F. Rinse the duck legs under cold running water to remove the salt and spices and pat dry with paper towels. Place them into a Dutch oven, cover with the duck fat, lard, or oil, and transfer the uncovered pot to the oven. Roast until the duck legs are fork-tender, 6 to 7 hours. Be sure to carefully monitor the temperature of the fat during cooking; it should remain at 190°F. When the duck legs are tender, remove them from the fat, and allow both the legs and the fat to cool enough to stop cooking. They

¼ cup kosher salt

1 tsp freshly cracked black pepper

2 tsp chopped thyme (or 1 tsp dried thyme)

2 bay leaves, crumbled

4 duck legs (about 3 lb), bone in, thighs and drumstick attached

1 qt duck fat, lard, or canola oil

can be used immediately or stored warm. To store, place the duck legs into a crock or bowl, cover completely with the cooled fat, and refrigerate for up to 4 months.

4. When ready to serve, preheat the oven to 350°F. Remove the duck legs from the fat. Add 1 to 2 tablespoons of the duck fat to an ovenproof pan and sear the skin side of the duck legs over medium-high heat until they are golden brown and crisp, about 2 minutes. Turn the legs over and place them in the oven until warmed through, about 12 minutes.

5 SIDES AND SALADS

After hours of low and slow cooking, braised, barbecued, and slow-roasted meats are a prize on their own. But paired with the perfect side dish or salad, they are the star on a plate full of flavors and textures.

THERE ARE MANY TRADITIONAL side dishes that hold their own against the richness of slow-cooked meats, like Classic Mac and Cheese (page 186), Spoonbread (page 205), and Boston Baked Beans (page 200). Whipped Potatoes (page 173) and Soft Polenta (page 203) are creamy comfort foods, at their best when drowning in the flavorful sauces of roasts and braises. And meat is not alone in receiving special treatment; cipollini onions, root vegetables, and potatoes are all roasted to bring out the sweet qualities that enhance the flavors of slow-cooked meats.

Cold side dishes and salads can be a refreshing addition to a barbecue menu, and often bring much needed acidity. Coleslaw (opposite) is a perfect accompaniment to tender, slow-cooked meats, and its variations offer a new take on this crunchy, tangy salad. Brussels Sprout Slaw (page 165), a mix of thinly shaved sprouts and Asian flavors, is a delicate but exciting way to enjoy a familiar dish. Roasted Pear and Arugula Salad with Caramelized Shallot Vinaigrette (page 191) is both sweet and sharp, with flavors that balance the rich items.

Coleslaw

This is a traditional mayonnaise-based coleslaw that works well as a side dish or on a barbecued pork butt sandwich. Salting the cabbage pulls out some of the moisture so that the dressing will not be too thin.

1. Combine the cabbage, onion, and carrot with the salt in a large bowl and toss. Fit a colander over another large bowl and transfer the vegetables to the colander to drain for at least 2 hours.

2. TO MAKE THE DRESSING: Combine the sour cream, mayonnaise, vinegar, mustard, sugar, and celery seeds in a bowl and whisk until the sugar has dissolved. The dressing can be stored for up to 3 days in the refrigerator.

3. When the vegetables have drained, lightly rinse them under cold running water. Allow any excess water to drain, then remove the vegetables from the colander, place them on a clean towel, and gently squeeze dry.

4. Combine the vegetables with the dressing, mix to coat, and refrigerate.

5. When well chilled, season the coleslaw with additional salt and pepper, as needed, and serve.

3 cups thinly sliced green cabbage

½ cup thinly sliced yellow onion

½ cup grated carrot

2 tsp kosher salt, plus more as needed

DRESSING

⅓ cup sour cream

⅓ cup mayonnaise

2 tbsp apple cider vinegar

1 tsp prepared mustard

1 tsp sugar

1 tsp celery seeds

Freshly cracked black pepper, as needed

CHEF'S NOTE

The coleslaw can be refrigerated in an airtight container for up to 4 days.

SIDES AND SALADS

Memphis-Style Mustard Coleslaw

MAKES 6 SERVINGS

Mustard is a very common accompaniment and flavoring in barbecue. This coleslaw is also known as "Tennessee mustard coleslaw," because it is commonly served with pork barbecue in that region.

1. Combine the cabbage, onion, carrot, and salt in a large bowl and toss together. Fit a colander over another large bowl, and transfer the vegetables to the colander to drain for at least 2 hours.

2. To MAKE THE DRESSING: Combine the mustard, ketchup, mayonnaise, vinegar, sour cream, sugar, celery seeds, if using, and cayenne and whisk until the sugar has dissolved. Refrigerate until needed.

3. Lightly rinse the drained vegetables under cold running water, drain any excess water, and pat dry on clean paper towels.

4. Combine the dressing and the vegetables and mix to coat the vegetables. Refrigerate until well chilled. Just before serving, taste the coleslaw and adjust the seasoning if needed as cold foods require more seasoning than warm foods. Serve chilled.

6 cups green cabbage, shredded (or one 16-oz bag coleslaw mix)

1 cup thinly sliced white onion

½ cup shredded carrot

2 tsp kosher salt

DRESSING

⅓ cup prepared yellow mustard

¼ cup ketchup

¼ cup mayonnaise

¼ cup apple cider vinegar

¼ cup sour cream

⅓ cup sugar

1 tsp celery seeds (optional)

Small pinch of cayenne pepper

Brussels Sprout Slaw

MAKES 6 SERVINGS

The thin Brussels sprout leaves give this Asian-inspired slaw a more delicate texture and appearance than a traditional cabbage slaw.

1. Remove any brown leaves from the outside of the Brussels sprouts and trim the bottoms. Using a slicing knife, stainless-steel French mandoline, or plastic Benriner mandoline, thinly slice each sprout, starting at the top and working toward the bottom. You will need about 6 cups of sliced Brussels sprouts.

2. Combine the mayonnaise, lime juice, fish sauce, and sugar in a bowl. Mix to incorporate, then stir in the peanuts, green onions, and cilantro. Toss the dressing with the Brussels sprouts. Refrigerate the slaw until chilled and serve.

2 lb Brussels sprouts

¾ cup mayonnaise

¼ cup fresh lime juice

2 tbsp plus 1 tsp fish sauce

2 tsp sugar

⅔ cup chopped raw peanuts

½ cup thinly sliced green onions

¼ cup chopped cilantro

SIDES AND SALADS

165

Braised Red Cabbage

The sweet, tangy flavor of red cabbage is a great accompaniment to pork dishes and roasted meats.

1. Preheat the oven to 350°F.

2. Heat the oil or bacon fat in a large pot over medium-low heat. Add the apples and onions and sweat them until the onions are translucent and the apples are slightly soft, about 5 minutes. Add the wine, vinegar, jelly, sugar, and 1 cup of the water.

3. Place the cinnamon stick, clove, bay leaf, and juniper berries onto a piece of cheesecloth, pull up the four corners of the cheesecloth, and tie it into a pouch. Add the sachet and the cabbage to the pot. Cover and transfer to the oven. Braise until the cabbage is tender, 15 to 20 minutes, checking regularly to be sure the liquids have not evaporated completely and adding more water if necessary. Remove and discard the sachet.

4. If desired, dissolve the cornstarch in the remaining ½ teaspoon cold water to make a slurry, and stir the mixture into the cabbage to thicken the cooking liquid slightly. Season with salt and pepper and serve immediately.

CHEF'S NOTE

This recipe may also be cooked in a slow cooker on high for 20 to 25 minutes.

1 tbsp vegetable oil or rendered bacon fat

2 cups peeled and diced Granny Smith apples

1¼ cups diced onion

3 tbsp red wine

3 tbsp red wine vinegar

3 tbsp red currant jelly or apple jelly

2 tbsp sugar

1 cup water, plus ½ tsp (optional), plus more as needed

1 cinnamon stick

1 clove

1 bay leaf

2 juniper berries

1 medium head red cabbage, sliced ⅛ inch thick

¾ tsp cornstarch (optional)

½ tsp kosher salt

¼ tsp freshly ground black pepper

Baked Vidalia Onions

Don't let the idea of eating a baked onion turn you off to this recipe. Vidalia onions are very sweet, and that sweetness intensifies when they are cooked. The butter and balsamic vinegar add even more sweetness when they mingle with the onions' natural juices.

6 medium Vidalia onions or any other sweet onion

1 tbsp kosher salt

1 tsp freshly cracked black pepper

1 tsp chopped rosemary

1 tsp thyme leaves

6 tbsp salted butter

6 tbsp balsamic vinegar

1. Preheat the oven to 375°F.

2. Peel the onions and trim the tops, removing about ½ inch. Trim the root end of the onions, being careful to remove only the root and to leave the core of the onion intact; the core is needed to hold the onion together after baking. Make 3 to 4 cuts across the top of each onion, cutting only two-thirds of the way down. This will create 6 to 8 wedges on the top two-thirds of the onion.

3. Place each of the onions, root end down, on a double layer of aluminum foil measuring approximately 12 inches by 12 inches. Sprinkle the onions with the salt, pepper, rosemary, and thyme. Top each onion with a tablespoon of the butter. Pull the foil up over each onion to create a pouch that leaves the top of the onion exposed. Pour 1 tablespoon of vinegar over the onion in each pouch. Seal the foil tightly to completely enclose each onion.

4. Place the foil-wrapped onions on a baking sheet and transfer them to the oven. Bake until the onions are very tender, about 1 hour. Remove from the oven and let rest for about 10 minutes before serving to allow the onions to cool and absorb some of the juices that escaped during baking.

5. This dish is best served in individual bowls slightly larger than the size of the onions. Carefully peel the foil back and pour the liquid from each pouch into a bowl. Using a spatula, place an onion into each bowl. Once in the bowls, the onions will open up and spread out like flowers.

Roasted Cipollini Onions

These onions are most flavorful when they are roasted under a meat that is smoking, such as Barbecued Beef Brisket (page 104) or pork ribs, so that the juices and fat from the meat drip onto the onions. The drippings baste and season the onions, making them a perfect match to serve with the meat. If you can't smoke-roast them, these onions are also great when roasted in the oven instead.

2 tbsp olive oil

12 unpeeled garlic cloves

8 sprigs thyme (or ½ tsp dried thyme)

1 lb cipollini or small boiling onions, peeled

Kosher salt, as needed

1. Combine the oil, garlic, and thyme. Add the onions and toss to coat with the oil.

2. Put the onions in a roasting pan, season with salt, and place the roasting pan under a meat item being cooked in a smoker about 1 hour before the meat is done, or place in the oven. The fat and juices from the meat will drip onto the onions, basting and seasoning them. (If you are not cooking the onions with a meat item, see the Chef's Notes.)

3. Each time you check the smoker, water pan, fuel, and so on, check the onions to make sure that they do not burn and that the roasting pan doesn't get too dry. If the pan is going dry, add a small amount of water to it. If the garlic starts to burn, remove and discard it.

4. Roast until the onions are translucent and very tender. The cooking time will vary depending on the size of the onions and the temperature of the smoker, but generally they should take about 1 hour to cook. Remove the onions from the oven, discard the garlic cloves, and serve as an accompaniment to the smoked meat.

CHEF'S NOTES

Oven Roasting Method Add 1 tablespoon of any dry rub for any meat (if dry rub is not available, substitute 1 teaspoon salt and ½ teaspoon freshly cracked black pepper) to the oil, garlic, and thyme before tossing with the onions. Place the onions into a roasting pan, cover, and place in a 375°F oven. After 10 minutes, remove the cover, stir the onions, and return the pan to the oven. Roast until the onions are translucent and very tender. The cooking time will vary depending on the size of the onions, but generally they should take about 30 minutes to cook.

When purchasing the onions for this recipe, try to find onions that are all similar in size.

Roasted Root Vegetables

MAKES 4 SERVINGS

Even if you don't favor root vegetables, I bet you'll enjoy these. Roasting reduces the moisture content of root vegetables, which concentrates their sweetness and flavor, and caramelizing the vegetables adds yet another level of flavor.

1. Preheat the oven to 400°F.

2. Wrap the beets in aluminum foil and roast them in the oven until they are tender, about 1 hour. Set aside to cool (see Chef's Notes).

3. Meanwhile, place the onions, parsnips, carrots, turnips, and garlic in a bowl and season with the rosemary, thyme, oil, vinegar, salt, and pepper. Toss to coat the vegetables, and pour them onto a baking pan. Transfer to the oven and roast, stirring the vegetables every 15 minutes. If any of the vegetables are cooking faster than the others, remove them when they are tender, and return the rest of the vegetables to the oven. Continue roasting until all of the vegetables are tender, about 45 minutes.

4. When the beets are cool to the touch, peel and dice them into 1-inch cubes. They should peel easily using a paper towel.

2 beets, red, golden, or both (about 2 inches in diameter)

1 cup halved pearl onions, peeled (see Chef's Notes)

1 cup diced parsnips

1 cup diced carrots

1 cup diced yellow or white turnips

6 unpeeled garlic cloves

2 sprigs rosemary

4 sprigs thyme

2 tbsp extra-virgin olive oil

1 tbsp balsamic vinegar

½ tsp kosher salt, plus more as needed

¼ tsp freshly cracked black pepper

5. When all of the vegetables are tender, remove the rosemary and thyme sprigs and combine the beets with the other vegetables. Remove the peels from the garlic and add to the mixture. Sprinkle lightly with kosher salt and serve.

CHEF'S NOTES

The onions will be a lot easier to peel if you blanch them first in boiling hot water for 2 minutes.

The beets are cooked separately because they would otherwise turn the rest of the vegetables pink. If you don't care about that, they can be cut raw and cooked along with the other vegetables. Choosing golden beets will prevent this problem.

It's important that all of the vegetables are diced to the same size. This will allow them all to cook at the same rate in the oven.

Oven-Roasted Potatoes

These crispy, herb-scented potatoes are simple to prepare and make a perfect accompaniment to roasted meats. The roasted garlic provides a great flavor contrast with the potatoes. I suggest making extra, because the leftovers are fantastic pan-fried.

1. Preheat the oven to 400°F.

2. Place the vegetable and olive oils in a 9- to 10-inch ovenproof pan. Add the potatoes and toss in the oils to coat. Add the garlic, rosemary, thyme, salt, and pepper and toss with the potatoes to coat. Cover the pan tightly with aluminum foil or a lid and transfer to the oven. Roast for 25 minutes.

3. Carefully uncover the pan and turn the potatoes over. Using a fork or skewer, check for tenderness; if the potatoes are nearly tender and the fork or skewer pulls out easily, return the potatoes to the oven, uncovered, just to crisp the skin, about 10 minutes. If they are not yet nearly tender, cover the pan tightly again and returning to the oven to roast for about 10 minutes more. When the potatoes are nearly tender, remove the cover and return the pan to the oven until the potatoes are fork-tender and the skins are crisp, about 10 minutes. If desired, sprinkle with a little more salt and pepper. Remove the peels from the garlic, add to the potatoes, and serve.

2 tbsp vegetable oil

2 tbsp extra-virgin olive oil

1½ to 2 lb unpeeled fingerling, Red Bliss, or yellow creamer potatoes (1½ to 2 inches long), washed well

10 unpeeled garlic cloves

2 sprigs rosemary (6 inches long)

6 sprigs thyme

2 tsp kosher salt, plus more as needed

1 tsp freshly cracked black pepper, plus more as needed

CHEF'S NOTE

Be careful not to overcook the garlic. If it is cooked before the potatoes, remove it and continue to cook the potatoes.

Whipped Potatoes

Although the word "whipped" captures these potatoes' airy consistency, the name is actually misleading. You should never whip potatoes, whether by hand, food processor, or an electric mixer, because overmixing will give them a starchy appearance and flavor. Rather, a food mill or ricer is perfect for preparing lump-free potatoes. If you don't have one, "mash" them by hand with a potato masher.

1. Wash the potatoes, peel them, and rinse them again. Cut them into 1½- to 2-inch slices. Place the potatoes in a pot with enough cold water to cover them by 2 inches and add the salt. Gradually bring the water to a simmer over medium heat. Simmer until the potatoes are easily pierced with a fork, 10 to 15 minutes. Drain the potatoes immediately and return them to the pan. Place the pan over low heat to dry the potatoes until no more steam rises from them. While they're still hot, use a food mill or ricer to purée the potatoes into a warmed bowl.

2. Add the butter and mix it into the potatoes by hand with a whisk or flexible spatula. Add the half-and-half and stir well to combine. If the potatoes are not a smooth, light consistency, add more half-and-half as needed. Taste and season with pepper, additional salt, and butter as needed. Serve immediately.

2 lb russet potatoes

2 tbsp kosher salt, plus more as needed

2 tbsp butter, soft but not melted, plus more as needed

¼ cup half-and-half, warm, plus more as needed

Freshly ground pepper, as needed

CHEF'S NOTE

To make Garlic Whipped Potatoes: Roast 5 or 6 unpeeled garlic cloves in a small baking dish in a 350°F oven until the flesh is soft and deep brown, about 20 minutes. Squeeze the garlic pulp from the skin and mash with a fork to make a paste. Purée along with the potatoes, blending well to distribute the garlic evenly.

Boiled Potatoes

If you keep a few key points in mind, it's simple to serve creamy, full-flavored boiled potatoes. First, select the proper type of potato (see Chef's Notes) and cut the potatoes into pieces of an appropriate, uniform size. It is also critical that you start with cold water, because if you start with boiling water, the potatoes will not cook uniformly. Finally, be very careful not to overcook the potatoes.

1. Rinse the potatoes. If you are not using small potatoes, cut them into a uniform size, but do not dice the potatoes into small chunks or they will absorb too much water. Rinse again, if needed, and place in a pot. Cover the potatoes with 2 inches of cold water.

2. Add the salt and bring to a boil over high heat, uncovered. Reduce the heat and gently boil the potatoes until they can be pierced with a skewer and the skewer slides out easily, 25 to 30 minutes.

3. Drain the potatoes immediately and transfer them to a warm bowl. Do not let the potatoes sit in the hot water or they will absorb excess moisture. Season the potatoes with pepper and additional salt, as needed, and, if desired, toss with the butter or oil and/or parsley or chives.

1½ lb new potatoes (see Chef's Notes), washed, peeled if desired

2 tbsp kosher salt, plus more as needed

Freshly cracked black pepper, as needed

Butter or extra-virgin olive oil, as needed (optional)

Chopped flat-leaf parsley or chives, as needed (optional)

Using the proper potato is always very important. For this recipe, you must use "new" potatoes. New potatoes are also referred to as "waxy" or "high-moisture, low-starch" potatoes. They are not a specific variety of potatoes but simply young potatoes that are harvested while still immature. Some examples are small Red Bliss potatoes, fingerling potatoes, and creamers. These potatoes tend to have thin, tender skins so they are most often cooked with the skins on, which helps to retain their flavor and hold their shape after cooking. New potatoes are good for boiling, low-and-slow cooking methods, and cold preparations; however, they are not the right choice for mashed or whipped potatoes due to their high moisture content.

If you are precooking potatoes for another dish, such as potato salad, do not shock them to cool, because they will absorb water, taste watery, and be difficult to deal with. Instead, drain the potatoes; arrange them in a single layer on a baking sheet to cool at room temperature, then chill.

Warm German Potato Salad

MAKES 6 SERVINGS

This is a classic European-style potato salad with a sweet-and-sour flavor. It is traditionally served warm, but it can also be served cold.

1. Place the potatoes in a 3-quart pot and fill with enough cold water to cover the potatoes with 3 inches of water. Add 2 tablespoons of the salt and bring to a boil over high heat. Reduce the heat and simmer gently until the potatoes are fork-tender, 30 to 40 minutes. Remove the pot from the heat and drain the potatoes well in a colander. While they are still warm, slice the potatoes into ½-inch disks and transfer them to a large bowl.

2. Meanwhile, in a 1-quart saucepan, cook the bacon over low to medium heat until it just starts to crisp, about 5 minutes. Add the chicken broth, vinegar, onion, sugar, mustard, and pepper to the bacon and bring to a simmer over medium heat. Simmer gently until the onions are tender, about 10 minutes. Remove the pan from the heat and season with the remaining 1 teaspoon salt.

2 lb (about 6 cups) yellow or Red Bliss potatoes, peeled if desired

2 tbsp plus 1 tsp kosher salt

5 slices bacon, cut into ½-inch pieces

½ cup chicken broth

⅓ cup distilled white vinegar

½ cup diced onion

¼ cup sugar

1 tsp prepared yellow mustard

½ tsp freshly ground black pepper

2 tbsp sliced chives

3. Pour the bacon-onion dressing over the warm potatoes, stirring gently to make sure the dressing gets absorbed as much as possible. Garnish with the chives and serve. The potatoes can be reheated in the microwave if necessary.

CHEF'S NOTE

It's important that you use "new potatoes" such as Red Bliss potatoes or yellow creamers and not baking or russet potatoes. See the Chef's Notes on page 175 for more information on new potatoes.

Boiled Root Vegetables

MAKES 4 SERVINGS

Like potatoes, other root vegetables, such as carrots, turnips, rutabagas, and parsnips, are a great accompaniment to many of the braised, stewed, and roasted dishes in this book. You can boil a single root vegetable for a simple side dish or combine a variety of different boiled root vegetables for beautiful color and flavor contrast. If you plan to combine several types of root vegetables, you can boil them separately or together; if you're boiling them together, be sure to cut all of the vegetables into a uniform size so that they will cook evenly. You can serve boiled root vegetables as described in this recipe, or blend them after boiling and serve them as a purée, like mashed potatoes.

1. Place the carrots in a pot and add enough cold water to cover them by 2 inches. Add the salt to the water and bring to a boil over high heat.

2. Reduce the heat and gently simmer the carrots until tender, about 15 minutes. After 15 minutes, remove a piece from the pot and apply pressure on it with a fork; if it feels tender, drain the carrots. If not, continue cooking until tender. Cooking times can vary widely depending on the type of root vegetable you are using and the size into which it is cut, but all root vegetables must be cooked until they are tender in order to develop the sweet flavor.

3. Season with pepper and additional salt, as needed, and, if desired, toss with butter or oil.

1 lb trimmed and peeled carrots (or other root vegetables), cut into uniform pieces

2 tbsp kosher salt, plus more as needed

Freshly cracked black pepper, as needed

Butter or extra-virgin olive oil, as needed (optional)

LOW AND SLOW

CHEF'S NOTES

To boil the vegetables ahead of time, follow the same cooking method except after the vegetables are drained, immediately spread them out into a single layer on a baking sheet to cool at room temperature. When the vegetables are cool, refrigerate them until you are ready to reheat and serve. To reheat, briefly plunge the vegetables into lightly salted, boiling water or quickly sauté them in a pan over medium heat with a small amount of butter or olive oil. For an added dimension of flavor, you can cook them a little longer in the sauté pan to slightly caramelize them. Adjust the seasoning with salt and pepper, if necessary, and serve.

If boiling onions, do not cut them into pieces. Boil them whole. Other root vegetables should be trimmed, peeled, and cut into uniform pieces before boiling.

Boiled Green Vegetables

MAKES 4 SERVINGS

Green vegetables get their beautiful color from chlorophyll. Chlorophyll is sensitive to acid and heat, so be sure to use lots of boiling salted water to cook green vegetables and do not add so many vegetables to the pot at once that you lose the boil. Cook the vegetables to the desired doneness and serve immediately. Most green vegetables, including the green beans used in this recipe, asparagus, and broccoli, should not sit for an extended period of time after cooking or they will lose their brilliant color and start to turn brown.

1. Place the water in a pot, and add the salt. Cover and bring to a rapid boil over high heat.

2. Remove the cover and add the green beans. Continue to boil, uncovered, until the beans reach the desired tenderness, about 5 minutes. The water should remain at a constant boil during cooking; it may be necessary to cook the vegetables in batches in order to maintain a boil.

3. To check for doneness, remove a bean from the water and taste it. Opinions vary on the level of tenderness desired in cooked vegetables; as a general rule, they should be "tender-crisp," that is, easy to bite but still pleasantly firm. When the beans are cooked to your likeness, drain them.

4. Season with pepper and additional salt, as needed, and serve immediately (see Chef's Notes).

2 qt water

2 tbsp kosher salt, plus more as needed

1 lb trimmed green beans (or other green vegetables)

Freshly cracked black pepper, as needed

LOW AND SLOW

CHEF'S NOTES

To make this dish ahead, you can use the precooking method. Follow the same cooking method, except when the vegetables are done cooking, drain them, and immediately shock them in a large bowl of ice water. Once the vegetables are cold, remove them from the ice water, and hold them in the refrigerator until you are ready to serve. Reheat the vegetables before serving by briefly plunging them into lightly salted boiling water. Alternatively, you can reheat the vegetables in a small amount of butter or olive oil in a sauté pan over medium heat or in the microwave. Adjust the seasoning with additional salt and pepper, if necessary, and serve.

You may want to toss the cooked vegetables in some olive oil, butter, or toasted nuts for additional flavor.

Boiled Red or White Vegetables

MAKES 4 SERVINGS

Cooking red and white vegetables in an acid solution helps retain the vivid color pigments of red vegetables and keeps white vegetables bright as the acid hinders oxidation. When boiling, add an acid, like vinegar or lemon juice, to a large quantity of salted water. Only a small quantity of acid is needed, and adding too much can give the vegetable a sour flavor. Cauliflower is used in this recipe, but you may choose to substitute another red or white vegetable; this method works well with vegetables such as salsify and beets.

1. Fill a pot with the water. Add the salt and the vinegar or lemon juice and cover. Bring the water to a boil over high heat. As soon as the water begins to boil, remove the cover and add the cauliflower.

2. Cook with the water at a gentle boil until the cauliflower reaches the desired tenderness. Opinions vary on when the vegetable is cooked enough; after it has been boiled for about 8 minutes, remove a floret and taste it. If the cauliflower is not cooked to your liking, continue to cook until the desired tenderness is reached. Drain immediately.

3. Season with pepper and additional salt, as needed, and toss with butter or olive oil, if desired.

2 qt cold water

2 tbsp kosher salt, plus more as needed

¼ cup vinegar or lemon juice

1 lb cauliflower, cut into florets about 2 inches in diameter

Freshly cracked black pepper, as needed

Butter or extra-virgin olive oil, as needed (optional)

CHEF'S NOTES

To make boiled vegetables ahead, follow the same cooking method except after draining the boiled vegetables, immediately transfer them to a large bowl of ice water. When the vegetables are cold, they can be removed from the ice water and held in the refrigerator until you are ready to serve them. To reheat, briefly plunge the vegetables into lightly salted boiling water or rewarm in a sauté pan over medium heat in a small amount of butter or olive oil. You could also reheat them in the microwave. Adjust the seasoning with additional salt and pepper, if necessary, and serve.

Beets are the red vegetable that is most commonly cooked using this method. Always boil the beets with the skins on and peel them after cooking.

Fresh Pasta

MAKES 1 LB 8 OZ PASTA DOUGH

Fresh pasta is fun and easy to make. When cooked it should have a tender, velvety texture unlike packaged pasta, which is served with a bite, or al dente. Preparing fresh pasta gives you complete control over the size and shape of the noodles. You can make pasta from all-purpose flour, as suggested in this recipe, or use a finely ground semolina or durum wheat flour if you prefer; you may need to add an extra teaspoon or so of water if you choose a different flour.

1. Prepare the pasta dough using the well method or food processor method:

   To prepare the dough using the well method: Combine the flour and salt in a large bowl. Make a well in the center and place the eggs into the well. Pull some of the flour into the eggs and use two forks to mix it, incorporating the flour little by little until the dough forms a shaggy mass. Place the mass of dough onto a cutting board or countertop and knead it with the palms of your hands until it forms a smooth, firm dough, 10 to 15 minutes. If it is not forming a smooth dough, add a few drops of water. Be careful, because it is very easy to add too much water, and the final dough needs to be firm and not sticky. Wrap the dough tightly in plastic wrap and allow it to rest for 1 hour at room temperature.

   To prepare the dough using the food processor method: Place the flour and salt into the bowl of a food processor. With the food processor running on low speed, add the eggs. When all the eggs have been

PASTA DOUGH

1 lb all-purpose flour

1 tsp kosher salt, plus more as needed

4 large eggs, whisked

Water, as needed

incorporated, stop the food processor and use a rubber spatula to mix the ingredients and scrape down the sides of the bowl. Pulse the food processor several more times until the mixture is the consistency of grainy sand. Pull out a nugget of the dough and work it in your hand; if it forms a firm smooth dough in your hand, then the mixing is complete. If the nugget is very dry and will not form a dough, then add a few drops of water and pulse the dough in the food processor again. Continue this testing process as necessary until the pasta forms a smooth, firm dough. Shape the dough into a ball, wrap the dough tightly in plastic wrap, and allow it to rest for 1 hour at room temperature.

2. After the pasta dough has rested, you will notice that it feels softer, because the flour has been hydrated with the water. Work in batches, by hand or using a pasta machine, to form the dough into the desired shape. Be sure to flour the pasta lightly so that it doesn't stick together.

3. The pasta can be cooked immediately, covered lightly with plastic wrap and refrigerated for up to 2 days, or wrapped and frozen for up to 1 month. If refrigerated or frozen, the dough must go directly from the refrigerator or freezer into the boiling water to be cooked.

4. For every pound of pasta, bring 1 gallon of water with ¼ cup of salt to a boil over high heat. Add the pasta and cook until tender. Remember that fresh pasta will cook much more quickly than dried pasta, and cooking times can vary greatly between different shapes and thicknesses of fresh pasta. Drain the pasta in a colander and serve.

Classic Mac and Cheese

MAKES 6 TO 8 SERVINGS

Macaroni and cheese is an all-American comfort food that is nearly always served at barbecue joints. This is a basic recipe that yields a fairly heavy, thick sauce. If you like a lighter, creamier macaroni and cheese, simply omit 1 or 2 tablespoons of the flour.

1. Preheat the oven to 375°F.

2. Bring 3 tablespoons of the salt and the water to a boil over high heat. Add the pasta and boil until it is tender but not completely cooked, 7 to 9 minutes. Drain the pasta in a colander.

3. While the pasta is cooking, melt the butter in a separate pot over medium heat. Stir in the flour, and cook, stirring, until there are no lumps and the mixture has cooked through, about 5 minutes. Be careful not to develop any brown color. Stir in the milk, paprika, and bay leaf. Increase the heat to establish a simmer, and simmer for 10 to 15 minutes, until the sauce has thickened. Remove and discard the bay leaf.

4. Add 4½ cups of the cheese to the sauce in batches, about 1 cup at a time, waiting until most of the cheese has melted before adding the next batch. Do not allow the sauce to boil. Add the Tabasco, pepper, and remaining 2 teaspoons salt.

3 tbsp plus 2 tsp kosher salt

2 qt water

8 oz elbow macaroni

3 tbsp butter

5 tbsp all-purpose flour

3 cups whole milk

½ tsp sweet or smoked Spanish paprika

1 bay leaf

5 cups shredded sharp cheddar cheese

¼ tsp Tabasco sauce

½ tsp freshly cracked black pepper

¼ cup panko bread crumbs

5. Combine the macaroni with the cheese sauce and mix well to coat. Pour the mixture into a 2-quart baking dish, and sprinkle with the remaining ½ cup cheese. Sprinkle the bread crumbs over the cheese, and transfer the baking dish to the oven. Bake until the cheese is bubbling around the edges and the bread crumb crust on top has become golden brown and crunchy, 20 to 30 minutes. Allow the mac and cheese to set for 5 to 10 minutes before serving.

CHEF'S NOTE

This basic recipe is a great starting point for endless variations. Try adding chopped smoked ham, the "burnt ends" from a pork butt or beef brisket (see Bark, Mr. Brown, or Burnt Ends, page 68), or cooked lobster meat. You can also replace some of the cheddar with blue cheese.

Creamy Pasta Salad

This is a mayonnaise-based pasta salad made special by a variety of contrasting textures and flavors.

1. Pour the salt into the water and bring to a boil over high heat. Add the pasta and cook until very tender, 1 to 2 minutes longer than indicated on the package instructions. Be sure that the pasta is fully cooked, not al dente, because the acids in the dressing will firm up the pasta; if it is even slightly undercooked, the pasta will seem tough and undercooked when it's served. Drain the cooked pasta in a colander and rinse thoroughly with cold water to cool it down.

2. While the pasta is cooling, make the dressing: Combine the artichoke hearts, black and green olives, sun-dried tomatoes, mayonnaise, vinegar, mustard, basil, and salt and pepper as needed.

3. Combine the dressing, pasta, and tuna, if using, and stir to mix well. Refrigerate, covered, until chilled before serving, up to 3 days. Once chilled, the pasta may absorb some of the dressing and need to be reseasoned with salt and pepper before serving.

¼ cup kosher salt, plus more as needed

1 gal water

6 oz dried pasta (see Chef's Note)

One 6-oz jar artichoke hearts, drained, cut in half lengthwise

¼ cup black olives, halved

¼ cup green olives, halved

¼ cup sun-dried tomatoes in oil, chopped

½ cup mayonnaise

2 tbsp red wine vinegar

1 tsp prepared mustard

1 tbsp chopped basil

Kosher salt, as needed

Freshly cracked black pepper, as needed

One 5-oz can tuna, packed in water, drained (optional)

CHEF'S NOTE

Any dried pasta will work with this recipe, but shells or elbows work particularly well.

Roasted Beet and Orange Salad

Any type of beets can be used, but this recipe calls for a combination of red and golden beets for their colorful appearance. Roasting the beets intensifies their flavor.

1. Preheat the grill or oven to 400°F. Trim the beet greens to 1 inch above each beet; if desired, reserve the greens for another use. It is not required that you purchase beets with tops; it is most important that you select beets of a uniform size, around 2 inches in diameter. Wash the beets thoroughly in cold water but do not peel them.

2. Sprinkle the beets with the oil and ½ teaspoon of the salt and toss together to coat. Wrap the beets completely with a double layer of aluminum foil and seal tightly on all sides. Try to spread out the beets so they are not touching in the foil packet. Place the packet on the grill and close the lid, or place it on a baking sheet and transfer to the oven. Roast, turning occasionally, until the beets are tender, about 1 hour (roasting time can vary depending on the size of the beets). When the beets are tender, remove them from the grill or oven, unwrap the foil, and let cool.

3. When the beets are cool enough to handle, wearing plastic gloves and using a paper towel, rub the skin off; it should peel off easily. Slice each beet into ½-inch-thick slices. Arrange the beet and orange slices on a serving platter.

4. Combine the extra-virgin olive oil, orange juice, vinegar, orange zest, pepper, and the remaining ½ tsp salt in a small bowl and stir to mix well. Pour the mixture over the beet and orange slices and serve.

4 red beets, 1½ to 2 inches in diameter

4 golden beets, 1½ to 2 inches in diameter

1 tbsp olive oil

1 tsp kosher salt

3 navel oranges, peeled and sliced into ½-inch slices

¼ cup extra-virgin olive oil

¼ cup fresh orange juice

2 tbsp red wine vinegar

2 tsp grated orange zest

¼ tsp freshly cracked black pepper

SIDES AND SALADS

189

Roasted Pear and Arugula Salad with Caramelized Shallot Vinaigrette

MAKES 6 SERVINGS

This attractive salad features the classic combination of pears, nuts, and blue cheese. It's very delicious as an appetizer and also makes a great entrée topped with a piece of grilled or hot smoked fish. (Omit the blue cheese if serving with fish.)

1. Preheat the oven to 375°F.

2. To make the pears: Combine the lemon juice, honey, and salt. Cut the pears in half lengthwise and remove the stem down to the core. Remove the core with a melon baller, and remove the tiny piece of skin at the blossom end of the pears. Combine the pears with the lemon mixture.

3. Line a baking sheet with aluminum foil. (You will never get the baking sheet clean if you don't use the foil.) Place a rack on top of the foil in the baking sheet, and place the pears, cut side up, on the rack, reserving the lemon juice mixture. Drizzle or brush each pear with a little of the lemon mixture, reserving a little bit for use during cooking, if possible. Transfer the baking sheet to the oven.

4. Roast until the pears are completely tender and slightly caramelized on top, about 40 minutes, depending on the size of the pear. If you have any remaining lemon mixture, brush the pears with it about halfway through the cooking time. Pierce the

ROASTED PEARS

Juice of 1 lemon

2 tbsp honey

½ tsp kosher salt

3 unpeeled Bartlett pears

VINAIGRETTE

3 tbsp vegetable oil

3 shallots, thinly sliced

3 tbsp sherry vinegar

3 tbsp extra-virgin olive oil

1 tbsp honey

Kosher salt, as needed

Freshly cracked black pepper

3 cups baby arugula

⅓ cup walnuts, toasted, chopped

⅓ cup blue cheese, crumbled

SIDES AND SALADS

191

pears with a skewer to check for doneness. Remove the pears from the oven and allow to cool to room temperature. Once cool, cut each pear into 3 slices.

5. **TO MAKE THE VINAIGRETTE:** Warm the oil in a pan over low heat. Add the shallots and cook until they are golden brown, about 15 minutes. Cook the shallots slowly and watch them very closely once they just start to brown; shallots can burn quickly. When they are golden brown, strain them from the oil and quickly transfer them to a plate lined with paper towels. Use two forks to spread out the shallots into a single layer so that they cool quickly. Reserve the oil in a bowl and allow it to cool to room temperature.

6. When the oil is cool, whisk in the vinegar, olive oil, honey, salt, and pepper. Add half of the shallots to the vinaigrette. Taste the dressing and adjust as necessary with additional honey and/or vinegar. It should be sweet, but if serving the salad with fish, you should make it a little more tart. Season with additional salt and pepper as needed, and chill in the refrigerator until ready to use.

7. Combine the pear slices, arugula, about ¼ cup of the vinaigrette, the walnuts, the remaining shallots, and blue cheese in a large bowl and toss to make sure that everything is evenly coated with the dressing. Taste, adjust the seasoning with additional salt and pepper as needed, and add more dressing if necessary.

8. To serve, pick the pear slices out of the bowl of salad, and place 3 slices onto each of 6 chilled plates. Divide the salad equally among the plates.

Roasted Corn and Jícama Salad

MAKES 6 SERVINGS

This is a fantastic salad to serve in midsummer when corn on the cob is at its peak. The salad's other ingredients provide contrasting textures and perfectly balance the sweetness of the corn.

1. Preheat the oven or grill to 400°F.

2. Trim off half of the stem of each ear of corn and trim the silk and leaves at the tip of each cob close to the kernels, leaving the rest of the husk in place. Discard any husk leaves that fall off the cobs. Place the ears of corn directly on the rack of the oven, or place on the grill and cover with the lid. Roast, turning the corn periodically, until the corn is tender, 25 to 30 minutes. The husks may turn black and some of the kernels may look toasted or a little dark, but that will add more roasted flavor; just be very careful not to burn the corn kernels. When tender, remove the corn from the oven or grill and set aside to cool.

3. When the corn is cool enough to handle, remove the husks; they should peel off easily and most of the silk will be removed with the husk. Using a sharp knife, slice the corn kernels off of the cobs and discard the cobs.

4. Combine the corn kernels with the jícama, green and red bell peppers, cilantro, lime juice, and oil. Season with salt and pepper.

5. Serve at room temperature, or refrigerate, covered, until chilled before serving, up to 2 days.

6 ears of corn

1 cup small-dice jícama

½ cup seeded and diced green bell peppers

½ cup seeded and diced red bell peppers

2 tbsp chopped cilantro leaves

¼ cup fresh lime juice

¼ cup extra-virgin olive oil

1 tsp kosher salt

½ tsp freshly cracked black pepper

CHEF'S NOTE

The flavor and sweetness of the corn can vary greatly. You may need to adjust the seasoning with a small quantity of sugar, and/or additional lime juice or cilantro.

Roasted Red Pepper and Olive Salad

MAKES 4 TO 6 SERVINGS

This makes a great summer salad when it can be made with fresh peppers that are in season and at their best. It can be served on its own or as an accompaniment to slow-roasted or barbecued main dishes. If you'd like, substitute yellow or green bell peppers or use a combination of colors.

1. Place each bell pepper onto a hot grill or gas burner. (If a grill or gas burner is not available, you can blacken them under an oven broiler instead.) Roast each pepper over the flame, turning it with tongs, until it is charred black on all sides. The skin should turn black on the entire surface, but be very careful not to burn the flesh of the peppers. Place the charred peppers into a bowl and tightly cover with plastic wrap, or place into a zip-close plastic bag. Set aside at room temperature until the peppers have cooled and the steam has loosened their skins, about 30 minutes.

2. Remove the peppers from the bowl or bag and, using paper towels, rub away the blackened skin. The peppers should still be red and have a smoky flavor. Do not rinse the peppers under water; this will rinse away the roasted flavor and much of the peppers' natural flavorful oils as well. Remove the stem, seeds, and ribs from the peppers and slice the peppers into ½-inch strips.

3. Combine the strips of pepper with the olives, onion, cheese, basil, garlic, vinegar, and oil, and season with salt and pepper. If necessary, adjust the flavor with additional oil and/or vinegar.

3 large red bell peppers

⅓ cup Kalamata olives, pitted, halved

⅓ cup thinly sliced red onion

½ cup freshly grated Parmesan

8 to 10 large basil leaves, torn into ½-inch pieces

1 tbsp minced garlic

2 tbsp balsamic vinegar

2 tbsp extra-virgin olive oil

Kosher salt, as needed

Freshly cracked black pepper, as needed

Watermelon and Cucumber Salad

This is a very refreshing summer salad that goes well with most barbecue dishes. The salad is nonfat, but it's packed with flavor and carries a little heat from the crushed red pepper flakes.

1. Soak the onion slices in ice water for 2 hours to soften the flavor and make them crisp.

2. Combine the vinegar, sugar, 1 tablespoon of the mint, and the red pepper flakes in a bowl and refrigerate while preparing the remaining ingredients.

3. Remove the onion from the ice water and pat dry with paper towels. Combine with the watermelon and cucumbers in a large bowl.

4. Wash the lettuce and remove the leaves, being careful to keep the leaves whole. When ready to serve, add the vinegar mixture to the melon and cucumbers and stir to coat. Arrange 2 lettuce leaves on each of 4 chilled plates to form a cup shape. Fill each of the lettuce leaf cups with watermelon and cucumber salad. Garnish each plate with the radishes and the remaining mint.

½ cup thinly sliced red onion

¼ cup rice wine vinegar

2 tbsp sugar

3 tbsp mint leaves, thinly sliced

¼ tsp crushed red pepper flakes

2 cups watermelon balls (see Chef's Notes)

1 cup thinly sliced seedless cucumbers, peel on

1 head Boston lettuce

3 tbsp julienned radish

CHEF'S NOTE

To make perfect balls from the watermelon flesh, press a melon baller tool, also known as a Parisian scoop, into the watermelon and twist it to remove the ball of melon. If you do not have a melon baller, or just want to save time, cut the watermelon into 1-inch cubes instead.

Duck Confit Salad with Poached Egg

Whenever you're preparing duck confit, you should seize the opportunity to prepare extra. The concept behind duck confit is preservation, and when properly sealed in a layer of fat, the confit can be kept in the refrigerator for months. This is a quick and simple entrée salad that is a great way to utilize duck confit that you may have stored in your refrigerator. If frisée lettuce is not available, you can use mixed baby greens instead.

1. Preheat the oven to 325°F.

2. Spread the walnuts in a single layer on a baking sheet and toast in the oven, about 10 minutes. Set aside to cool. Increase the oven temperature to 350°F.

3. Heat the duck fat in an ovenproof sauté pan over medium-high heat. Add the duck legs and sear on both sides until crisp, about 2 minutes per side. Transfer the pan to the oven until the duck is heated through, 10 to 12 minutes.

4. In a shallow pan, combine the water and vinegar. The vinegar is important because it helps to quickly firm up the egg whites in order to give the finished eggs a nice shape. Bring the water to 180°F over low to medium heat.

5. Crack the eggs into individual custard cups. While swirling the water inside the pan with a wooden spoon, gently slide the eggs into the water and let them cook until the white is cooked and the yolk is the desired doneness, 6 to 8 minutes. Work in small

¼ cup walnuts

1 tbsp duck fat from Duck Confit (page 159)

4 Duck Confit legs (page 159)

2 qt water

⅓ cup white vinegar

4 large eggs

4 cups frisée lettuce

1 cup julienned apples

¼ cup dried cranberries

½ cup Lemon Vinaigrette (page 209)

batches, if necessary, to avoid overcrowding the pan. Be sure to keep the water temperature between 160° and 185°F at all times. Do not allow the water to simmer or boil, and remember that the more eggs you add at a time, the more the water temperature will drop.

6. Using a slotted spoon, remove the eggs from the water and gently pat dry with a clean towel.

7. Place the frisée in a bowl with the apples, cranberries, and walnuts. Add the lemon vinaigrette and toss to coat.

8. To serve, arrange about 1 cup of salad in the center of each plate or bowl. Add a crispy duck leg and a poached egg.

CHEF'S NOTE

If you'd like to poach the eggs ahead of time, remove the eggs from the poaching water and immediately plunge them into ice water to stop the cooking process. When ready to serve, reheat them in 180°F water without any vinegar.

Watercress Salad with Horseradish Vinaigrette

Watercress and horseradish have both been paired traditionally with roast beef and smoked meats. This salad can bring out the best of these classic combinations when served with beef.

1. Trim any long stems from the watercress and thoroughly wash it. Carefully dry it in a salad spinner; it bruises very easily.

2. **TO MAKE THE VINAIGRETTE:** Combine the horseradish, shallot, oil, and vinegar in a large bowl, and season with salt and pepper. Gently toss the watercress in the vinaigrette just prior to serving.

CHEF'S NOTE

Prepared hot horseradish may be substituted for fresh horseradish. The potency of horseradish, whether fresh or prepared, can vary widely, so you may find yourself needing much more or less horseradish than is called for here.

3 bunches watercress

VINAIGRETTE

2 tbsp peeled and grated fresh horseradish (see Chef's Note)

1 tbsp finely diced shallot

¼ cup extra-virgin olive oil

2 tbsp red wine vinegar

Kosher salt, as needed

Freshly ground black pepper, as needed

Boston Baked Beans

Baked beans are a standard side dish at most barbecue joints, because beans go with all sorts of barbecued dishes. This is a classic New England recipe that tastes best when made a day ahead and then reheated. Serve it as a side dish, use it to make baked bean sandwiches, or stir in sliced hot dogs for "franks and beans."

1. Soak the beans overnight in 2 quarts of cold water. Alternatively, quick soak them: Place the beans in a pot and cover with 3 quarts of cold water. Do not add any salt; this will toughen the beans. Bring to a boil over high heat, then reduce the heat and simmer for 5 minutes. Turn off the heat, cover, and allow the pot to sit for 1 hour. Drain the beans, and reserve the soaking water.

2. Preheat the oven to 300°F. Place the bacon, onion, and drained beans in the bottom of an ovenproof clay bean pot (one that is safe for stovetop use as well; use a head diffuser if necessary) or any oven-safe pot, or in a slow cooker.

3. In a separate pot, bring the molasses, brown sugar, mustard powder, bay leaf, and 3½ cups of the bean soaking water to a boil over high heat. Reduce the heat to establish a simmer, and simmer for 2 minutes. Pour the mixture over the beans.

4. Bring the bean mixture to a simmer over medium-high heat, cover, and transfer to the oven. Or, if using a slow cooker, cover and bring the beans to a

1 lb dried great northern or navy beans

3 slices bacon, chopped

¾ cup chopped onion

½ cup molasses

2 tbsp packed dark brown sugar, plus more as needed

1 tbsp dry mustard powder

1 bay leaf

⅓ cup ketchup, plus more as needed

¼ cup apple cider vinegar

1 tsp kosher salt

½ tsp freshly ground black pepper

low simmer. Check the pot every 30 to 45 minutes; if the liquid has reduced below the beans, add more water to keep them covered. Beans cannot cook without liquid. Cook until the beans are completely tender, 3½ to 4 hours, then stir in the ketchup and vinegar. (Acid will firm up the beans, so be sure that the ketchup and vinegar are not added until the beans are completely tender.) Remove and discard the bay leaf. Season with salt and pepper, and adjust the seasoning as needed with additional sugar and/or ketchup.

CHEF'S NOTE

Cook these beans, uncovered, in a smoker to give them a slightly smoky flavor. You can also place the beans under ribs or a pork butt during smoking to allow the beans to gain some barbecue flavor from the drippings.

Rice Pilaf

Pilaf is a simple style of cooking rice that is a foolproof way to ensure light fluffy individual grains and avoid sticky rice. Pilaf is a popular cooking method for rice and other grains throughout the world. This recipe calls for converted long-grain rice, but other grains, such as barley, quinoa, and millet, are also commonly used.

1. Preheat the oven to 350°F.

2. Warm the butter or oil in a 1-quart, medium-gauge, ovenproof pot over low heat. Add the onion, cover the pot with a lid, and sweat for 10 minutes. Properly sweated onions should be soft and translucent but not browned.

3. Remove the cover, increase the heat to medium-high, and stir in the rice. Cook, stirring constantly, for 1 minute. Add the water or broth, bay leaf, thyme, and salt and season with pepper, then bring the mixture to a simmer.

4. Cover the pot with a lid and transfer it to the oven. Bake for 18 minutes. Remove the pot from the oven and allow it to rest, still covered, for 5 minutes.

5. Remove the lid and remove and discard the bay leaf. Fluff the rice lightly with a fork, and serve.

2 tbsp butter or oil

¼ cup minced onion

1 cup long-grain white converted rice (such as Uncle Ben's)

2 cups water or chicken broth, warmed

1 bay leaf

1 sprig thyme

1 tsp kosher salt

Freshly cracked black pepper, as needed

CHEF'S NOTE

To make saffron rice pilaf: Add a pinch of saffron to the cooking liquid along with the bay leaf, salt, and pepper. Follow the same cooking method as described above.

Soft Polenta

MAKES 4 SERVINGS

Polenta is a great side dish for roasted and braised items. This is the soft version of cooked polenta and is served by spooning it onto the plate in much the same fashion as mashed potatoes. Leftovers can be chilled and then sliced into pieces to be grilled or pan-fried the next day.

1. Bring the water to a boil in a heavy saucepan over high heat. Add the salt.

2. To keep the polenta from becoming lumpy, add the cornmeal to the boiling water very gradually in a thin, steady stream, stirring constantly with a whisk until all of the cornmeal has been added.

3. Reduce the heat to low and simmer, stirring often with a wooden spoon, until the polenta has a smooth and velvety texture, about 45 minutes.

4. Taste the polenta to check for doneness; if it still feels coarse, add some water and continue cooking until it has a velvety, gelatin-like feeling on your palate when you taste it. You may need to add more water if it gets too thick.

5. Remove the pot from the heat and quickly stir in the butter and cheese. Serve immediately.

5 cups water

1½ tsp kosher salt

1 cup cornmeal

2 tbsp butter

½ cup freshly grated Parmesan

SIDES AND SALADS

203

Cornbread

You can't have barbecue without cornbread! It also pairs well with many slow-roasted and braised dishes. This is a basic cornbread recipe that is slightly sweet and perfect for creating hundreds of variations. Try adding jalapeños, cheddar cheese, chives, crumbled bacon, cooked sausage, honey, buttermilk, whole kernel or cream-style corn, or cooked black-eyed peas.

1. Preheat a 10-inch cast-iron skillet in a 400°F oven.

2. Meanwhile, combine the cornmeal, flour, sugar, baking powder, and salt in a bowl.

3. In a separate bowl, whisk together the eggs, milk, and ¼ cup of the oil or shortening until smooth.

4. When the pan is hot, pour the wet ingredients into the dry ingredients and gently fold them together using a rubber spatula. Do not overmix; it's okay if there are a few lumps left in the mixture. Once combined, the batter should be a pourable consistency. If it isn't thin enough to pour, add a couple teaspoons of milk.

5. Remove the pan from the oven and grease it with the remaining 2 tablespoons oil or shortening. Fill the pan with the batter and place it back into the oven. Bake until the top of the cornbread is lightly browned, the sides have started to pull away from the pan, and a toothpick comes out cleanly when inserted into the center, 25 to 30 minutes.

6. Serve warm or at room temperature.

1½ cups cornmeal

½ cup all-purpose flour

½ cup sugar

1½ tsp baking powder

1 tsp kosher salt

2 large eggs

1¼ cups whole milk, plus more as needed

¼ cup plus 2 tablespoons corn oil, canola oil, or vegetable shortening

Spoonbread

Spoonbread, which is popular in the southeastern United States, is similar to cornbread but with a lighter, airier consistency that necessitates that the side dish be "spooned" onto a plate. Like a soufflé, spoonbread should be served as soon as it comes out of the oven, before it has had a chance to deflate. Serve it anytime you would serve cornbread, particularly to accompany lamb and pork.

1. Preheat the oven to 375°F. Butter an 8-inch by 8-inch pan or a 1½-quart soufflé dish with 1 teaspoon of the butter. Add 1 tablespoon of the cornmeal to the pan and shake until the bottom and sides of the pan are coated with cornmeal.

2. Combine the milk, cream, and remaining 1 tablespoon butter in a medium sauce pot and bring to a simmer over medium-high heat. Slowly whisk in the remaining 1 cup cornmeal and the salt in a steady stream. Continue simmering the mixture over medium heat, stirring constantly, for 5 minutes. Remove the pot from the heat, and stir in the corn kernels and baking powder. Whisk in the egg yolks, one at a time, until they are incorporated.

3. In a nonreactive bowl, whisk the egg whites until they become frothy. Slowly whisk in the sugar, and continue whisking until you achieve soft peaks. Stir one-fourth of the egg whites into the cornmeal mixture. In three additions, gently fold in the remaining egg whites.

4. Pour the mixture into the prepared pan or soufflé dish and smooth out the top. Bake in the oven until the spoonbread has puffed and is golden brown, 35 to 40 minutes. Serve immediately.

1 tbsp plus 1 tsp salted butter

1 cup plus 1 tbsp cornmeal

2½ cups whole milk

½ cup heavy cream

2 tsp kosher salt

1 cup corn kernels, fresh or canned

1½ tsp baking powder

3 large eggs, separated

1 tbsp sugar

Smoked Seafood Salad

MAKES 6 SERVINGS

The instructions below are for serving this dish as a dinner entrée, but it can also be served as a lunch entrée, side salad, plated appetizer, or on cucumber slices as an hors d'oeuvre.

1. Prepare the seafood chunks by trimming off any skin from the fish. If there is a fatty gray area under the skin, scrape that off, and remove any bones with tweezers. If there are any large thick chunks, cut them to the same thickness as the other pieces.

2. Smoke the fish following the same process used to prepare Hot Smoked Salmon (page 129).

3. During the cooking process, if any pieces are cooking more quickly than the others, remove them when they are done and allow the remaining fish to finish cooking. Let cool.

4. When the fish is cool, flake it into chunky pieces. Add the artichokes, olives, tomatoes, sugar, shallot, lemon juice, oil, mustard, salt, and pepper. Gently stir the mixture with a rubber spatula until well combined. Taste and adjust the seasoning as necessary. Refrigerate until chilled.

2 to 2½ lb seafood chunks (see Chef's Note)

12 oz marinated artichokes, halved

⅓ cup Kalamata olives, pitted, sliced into quarters

¼ cup chopped sun-dried tomatoes in oil

1 tbsp sugar

1 tsp minced shallot

¼ cup fresh lemon juice

¼ cup extra-virgin olive oil

1 tbsp prepared Dijon or yellow mustard

1 tsp kosher salt

¼ tsp freshly cracked black pepper

2 lb cooked and chilled asparagus (follow the method for Boiled Green Vegetables on page 180)

6 to 12 leaves Boston lettuce

5. Divide the asparagus evenly among 6 plates. Place 1 or 2 lettuce leaves onto each plate. Gently stir the chilled salad, and divide it evenly among the plates, arranging it on top of the lettuce leaves.

CHEF'S NOTE

Fish markets and supermarkets will often sell "seafood chunks" at a reasonable price. These are cubes and other trimmings left over from the portioning of fish. If you don't see them, just ask at the fish counter. Most types of seafood and fish will work for this recipe; just avoid flaky, high-moisture fish like codfish. Some prime options are salmon, tuna, whitefish, halibut, and swordfish.

Smoked Salmon Spread

MAKES 1¼ CUPS SPREAD

This spread can also double as a smoked salmon dip for hors d'oeuvre. It's delicious on crackers, toast points, carrots, cucumber slices, apple slices, and so on. It's also an excellent way to use up scraps or leftovers from Hot Smoked Salmon.

1. Using a fork, mash the smoked salmon; try to get the salmon as smooth as possible.

2. Add the cream cheese, mayonnaise, and dill and stir to combine (see Chef's Notes).

3. Season with salt and pepper. The spread can be stored, covered, in the refrigerator for up to 1 week; do not freeze.

1 cup Hot Smoked Salmon (page 129)

3 tbsp cream cheese

3 tbsp mayonnaise

1 tsp chopped dill

Kosher salt, as needed

Freshly cracked black pepper, as needed

CHEF'S NOTES

If necessary, adjust the amount of cream cheese and/or mayonnaise to reach the consistency you like. You'll want the consistency thicker to use it as a spread and a little softer to serve it as a dip. Keep in mind that the spread will get thicker when it's refrigerated.

Don't be afraid to experiment with additional seasonings such as horseradish, chopped fresh chives, cayenne pepper, fresh lemon juice, and the like.

LOW AND SLOW

Lemon Vinaigrette

MAKES ¾ CUP

This dressing is simple to make and goes well with most any lettuce, particularly Boston or Bibb. It is a sweet-and-sour dressing. The balance between the sweet and sour may need to be slightly adjusted each time you make it depending on the tartness of the lemons.

1. Zest the lemons with the finest side of a box grater or using a rasp grater. Cut the lemons in half and juice them, straining out the seeds.

2. Combine the zest, ¼ cup plus 1 teaspoon of the lemon juice, the corn or canola oil, olive oil, and sugar and mix well. Season with salt and pepper. Taste the dressing with a piece of lettuce, and adjust the sweet-sour balance with additional lemon juice or sugar if necessary.

2 lemons

½ cup corn oil or canola oil

1 tbsp extra-virgin olive oil

1 tbsp plus 1½ tsp sugar

Kosher salt, as needed

Freshly cracked black pepper, as needed

CHEF'S NOTE

It is critical to use freshly squeezed lemon juice for this recipe. The fresh lemon flavor will deteriorate after several days, so make the dressing the day it is needed. It can be refrigerated for up to 1 week in an airtight container. After that point the freshness and lemon flavor is lost.

Red Wine and Roasted Garlic Vinaigrette

MAKES 1 CUP

Roasting garlic transforms any harshness into a very pleasant, sweet flavor. This sweetness from the roasted garlic balances and mellows the basic vinaigrette flavors in this recipe. Use it as a dressing for any salad greens.

1. Preheat the oven to 350°F.

2. Roast the garlic inside its skin: Rub the outside of each clove lightly with canola oil and wrap the garlic loosely in aluminum foil. Place the foil package on a baking sheet in the oven and roast until it is very tender and sweet, about 30 minutes. Allow the garlic to cool, then peel and chop it.

3. Combine the garlic with the vinegar, canola oil, olive oil, sugar, salt, and pepper. Refrigerate until chilled. Taste with a lettuce leaf, and adjust the seasoning as needed.

3 unpeeled garlic cloves

⅓ cup canola oil, plus more as needed

⅓ cup red wine vinegar

⅓ cup extra-virgin olive oil

1 tbsp sugar

½ tsp kosher salt

¼ tsp freshly cracked black pepper

CHEF'S NOTES

To make red wine vinaigrette, omit the garlic.

To use with Oven-Roasted Potatoes (page 172), prepare the oven-roasted potato recipe as directed, slice the potatoes into ½-inch disks, and add this vinaigrette to the warm potatoes. Serve as is, or chill before serving.

Almond-Fig Vinaigrette

MAKES 2 CUPS

This versatile vinaigrette can be used to create a salad with almost any type of greens. Figs and duck are a classic combination, so this recipe is especially delicious in salads that include duck confit or roasted duck or duck legs.

1. Preheat the oven to 325°F. Place the almonds on a baking pan and toast in the oven until a very light golden color, about 10 minutes. Remove the almonds from the pan and set aside to cool. When cool, chop into smaller pieces if needed.

2. Combine the vinegar, wine, shallots, almonds, and salt and pepper as needed in a bowl. Whisk in the olive and almond oils. Stir in the figs and lemon juice. If necessary, adjust the seasoning with additional salt and pepper. Refrigerate in an airtight container until ready to use.

¼ cup chopped almonds

⅓ cup balsamic vinegar

⅓ cup red wine

2 shallots, minced

Kosher salt, as needed

Freshly ground black pepper, as needed

1 cup olive oil (not extra-virgin)

¾ cup almond oil

½ cup chopped dried figs

Juice of 2 lemons

CHEF'S NOTE

The vinaigrette can be refrigerated in an airtight container for up to 2 weeks.

6 SAUCES AND RUBS

Making your own sauces and rubs is a simple way to add flavor and personality to your slow-cooked meat dishes. Whether it is simple Tomato Sauce (page 227) or zesty Apple-Horseradish Cream (page 222), a sauce or a rub can quickly and easily change the flavor profile of a dish.

SAUCES IN THIS CHAPTER are often regional recipes, influenced by local flavors and ingredients. The herbaceous Chimichurri Sauce (page 228), popular in Argentina, is typically served atop grilled meat. But replaced with tropical Pineapple Salsa (page 230), that same piece of meat is transported to the Caribbean, or to the Far East with Asian-Style Dipping Sauce (page 221).

Barbecue sauces take on different personalities throughout the United States and can transform the flavors of a rich, slow-cooked meat. The versatile Classic Barbecue Sauce (page 216) is sweet and thick, the tangy flavors of Carolina Mustard Sauce (page 219) pair perfectly with pork, and the whiskey-flavored Jack Black Barbecue Sauce (page 218) is sweet, sour, and good on everything.

Dry Rub for Beef

MAKES ½ TO ¾ CUP

This rub is perfect for beef, but it also works well on other meats, such as lamb or pork. Use about 1 tablespoon of rub per pound of meat. Sprinkle the meat with the rub and gently massage it into the meat.

Combine the sugar, salt, black pepper, cumin, smoked paprika, medium-hot paprika, garlic powder, onion powder, and cayenne.

¼ cup sugar

3 tbsp kosher salt

2 tbsp freshly cracked black pepper

2 tbsp freshly ground cumin

2 tbsp smoked Spanish paprika

2 tbsp medium-hot paprika

1 tbsp garlic powder

1 tbsp onion powder

½ tsp cayenne pepper

CHEF'S NOTE

The rub can be stored in a plastic bag for up to 6 months. If you can vacuum seal the bag, the rub will stay fresh longer.

Barbecue Dry Rub

The dry rubs for barbecued meats that appear in recipes throughout the book are tailored to produce a specific style of barbecue that honors the region from which it hails. This rub is simple and versatile, and can be customized to fit a variety of flavor profiles, so feel free to experiment.

Combine the paprika, chili powder, salt, cumin, sugar, mustard, black pepper, thyme, oregano, and cayenne.

CHEF'S NOTE

The rub can be stored in a plastic bag for up to 6 months. If you can vacuum seal the bag, the rub will stay fresh longer.

½ cup sweet paprika

¼ cup chili powder

2 tbsp kosher salt

1 tbsp ground cumin

2 tbsp sugar

1 tbsp dry mustard powder

2 tsp freshly ground black pepper

2 tbsp dried thyme

2 tbsp dried oregano

1 tsp cayenne pepper

SAUCES AND RUBS

Classic Barbecue Sauce

This is a classic mild, sweet-style barbecue sauce with a very slight acidity that gives the flavor balance. It is a good, thick, general-use, red barbecue sauce that works well with chicken, beef, and pork.

1. Heat the oil in a sauce pot over medium heat. Add the onion, reduce the heat to low, and cover the pot with a lid. Cook until the onions are translucent but not brown, about 4 minutes.

2. Add the ketchup, vinegar, molasses, brown sugar, mustard, garlic powder, cayenne, salt, and pepper, and increase the heat to establish a simmer. Simmer the sauce for 10 minutes. Adjust the consistency of the sauce if needed by adding the water. (If you plan to use this sauce to brush a meat while it's cooking, then keep the sauce thin by adding more water.)

3. Strain the sauce through a fine-mesh sieve. Use it immediately or refrigerate it until needed. The sauce can be refrigerated in an airtight container for up to 4 weeks.

2 tbsp corn oil

½ cup minced onion

2 cups ketchup

¼ cup apple cider vinegar

¼ cup molasses

¼ cup packed brown sugar

2 tbsp prepared yellow mustard

½ tsp garlic powder

Pinch of cayenne pepper

½ tsp kosher salt

½ tsp freshly ground black pepper

½ cup water, plus more as needed

Tangy Barbecue Sauce

MAKES 3 CUPS SAUCE

This sauce does double duty as both a dipping sauce and a glaze. It's unusual because it doesn't contain any sugar, so it is quite tart and tasty. It's a great complement to all meats.

1. Combine the butter, onion, and garlic in a 2-quart saucepan. Cook over medium heat until the butter melts and the onion and garlic just start to cook. Reduce the heat to low, cover the pot with a tight-fitting lid, and cook until the onions become transparent, about 10 minutes.

2. Add the vinegar, ketchup, broth or water, tomato paste, Worcestershire sauce, Tabasco, and salt and bring the mixture to a boil over high heat. Reduce the heat to establish a simmer, and simmer for 20 minutes. Strain the sauce to remove the onion and garlic pieces.

3. The sauce can be refrigerated in an airtight container for up to 2 weeks.

3 tbsp butter or margarine

⅓ cup minced onion

2 tbsp minced garlic

1 cup apple cider vinegar

1 cup ketchup

1 cup beef broth or water

⅓ cup tomato paste

1 tbsp Worcestershire sauce

1½ tsp Tabasco sauce

1 tsp kosher salt

Jack Black Barbecue Sauce

The name "Jack Black" refers to the Jack Daniels whiskey in the recipe and the deep color of the sauce. When it has finished cooking, the sauce may look burnt, but it isn't; the color is supposed to be very dark, and the sauce will actually turn black when brushed on a product and heated. It can be thinned with water and used as a glaze on pork ribs or other meats, or used as a dipping sauce.

1. Heat the oil in a 1-quart saucepan over medium heat. Add the onion and garlic to the oil and cover the pot with a lid. Cook the onion and garlic over low heat until translucent but not browned, about 10 minutes.

2. Add the chili powder and cayenne to the pan and stir into the oil for a few seconds. Add the tomato paste, ketchup, vinegar, Worcestershire sauce, coffee, whiskey, and sugar, and increase the heat to establish a simmer. Simmer for about 10 minutes. If you want to use the sauce as a glaze while barbecuing, serve it as is or thin it out with a little water if it is too thick. If you want a heavier dipping sauce, keep simmering the sauce until it has reduced to the desired thickness.

3. Strain the sauce through a fine-mesh sieve, and serve immediately or refrigerate until needed. The sauce can be refrigerated in an airtight container for up to 2 weeks.

1 tbsp canola oil

½ cup roughly chopped onion

1 tbsp finely chopped garlic

1 tbsp chili powder

¼ tsp cayenne pepper

½ cup tomato paste

½ cup ketchup

½ cup apple cider vinegar

½ cup Worcestershire sauce

½ cup black coffee

¼ cup Jack Daniel's whiskey

¼ cup packed brown sugar

Water, as needed (optional)

CHEF'S NOTE

This is a sweet-and-sour–style barbecue sauce with moderate heat. If you prefer a spicier sauce, add more cayenne or substitute a half-sharp or hot paprika. If you prefer a milder sauce, omit the cayenne.

Carolina Mustard Sauce

MAKES 1½ CUPS SAUCE

This sauce is a product of South Carolina's large German population and their affinity for mustard. It is an extremely easy barbecue sauce to make because it doesn't require any cooking. It works very well as a dipping sauce for pork, but it can basically be used however you like.

Combine the mustard, honey, vinegar, ketchup, Worcestershire sauce, sugar, cayenne, and black pepper and mix well. Refrigerate overnight before serving. The sauce can be refrigerated in an airtight container for up to 4 weeks.

¾ cup prepared yellow mustard

½ cup honey

¼ cup apple cider vinegar

2 tbsp ketchup

2 tsp Worcestershire sauce

1 tbsp packed brown sugar

Small pinch of cayenne pepper

⅛ tsp freshly ground black pepper

Western Carolina Dipping Sauce

This is a thin dipping sauce that works well with all barbecued pork and can be used in place of the vinegar sauce on barbecued pulled pork.

Combine the vinegar, ketchup, sugar, salt, black pepper, and red pepper flakes and mix well. Refrigerate in an airtight container until needed, up to 4 weeks.

1½ cups apple cider vinegar

¾ cup ketchup

3 tbsp packed brown sugar

1½ tsp kosher salt

1½ tsp freshly cracked black pepper

½ tsp crushed red pepper flakes

Asian-Style Dipping Sauce

This is a fantastic thick black dipping sauce that is very easy to make. It is extremely versatile, so serve it with everything!

1. Combine the hoisin sauce, soy sauce, honey, vinegar, sesame oil, Sriracha, sugar, and ginger in a 1-quart saucepan and bring the mixture to a boil over high heat. Reduce the heat to establish a gentle simmer and simmer for 5 minutes, stirring constantly.

2. Serve the sauce immediately, or chill in the refrigerator to serve cold. The sauce can be refrigerated in an airtight container for up to 3 months.

1 cup hoisin sauce

½ cup soy sauce

¼ cup honey

¼ cup rice wine vinegar

1 tbsp sesame oil

¾ tsp Sriracha sauce

¼ cup packed brown sugar

1 tsp ground ginger

Apple-Horseradish Cream

MAKES 1 CUP SAUCE

Horseradish and smoke are a match made in heaven. This creamy horseradish sauce goes well with most any smoked fish served cold.

1. In a chilled bowl, whisk the heavy cream until it forms medium peaks.

2. Gently fold the sour cream into the whipped cream, then fold in the apples, horseradish, and salt. Refrigerate until needed. The sauce can be made several hours ahead, but it will not hold overnight, since the salt will pull moisture from the apples and make the sauce watery.

¼ cup heavy cream

⅓ cup sour cream

¼ cup peeled and grated Granny Smith apples (see Chef's Notes)

3 tbsp prepared hot horseradish, drained (see Chef's Notes)

¼ tsp kosher salt

CHEF'S NOTES

Green apples, like Granny Smiths, are preferred for this recipe since they are less likely to brown due to oxidation.

Fresh horseradish may be substituted for prepared horseradish. The potency of horseradish, whether fresh or prepared, can vary widely, so you may find yourself needing much more or less than is called for here.

LOW AND SLOW

Creamy Horseradish Sauce

This sauce is a nice complement to any smoked chicken or fish that is served cold. It can also be used as a dressing for chicken or seafood salad, particularly if the meats are smoked.

Combine the sour cream, mayonnaise, horseradish, vinegar, salt, and pepper in a bowl and stir to combine. Refrigerate in an airtight container until needed, up to 1 week.

½ cup sour cream

½ cup mayonnaise

2 tbsp prepared hot horseradish (see Chef's Note)

½ tsp white wine vinegar

½ tsp kosher salt

¼ tsp freshly ground black pepper

CHEF'S NOTE

The potency of horseradish, whether prepared or fresh, can vary widely, so you may find yourself needing much more or less than is called for here.

Lentil Ragout

This recipe works as both a sauce and a salad. If serving as a sauce, it may be necessary to thin it with a little broth or water. If serving it as a salad, a little more lemon juice or salt may be needed. Always be sure to adjust the seasoning after chilling the salad, because cold foods tend to convey less flavor than hot foods.

1. Sift through the lentils to check for rocks and dirt. Wash the lentils thoroughly.

2. Heat the oil and bacon in a sauce pot over low heat. Add the onion, celery, carrot, and garlic, cover the pot, and cook the vegetables until the onions are translucent, about 10 minutes.

3. Remove the lid and stir in the tomato paste. Add the broth, lentils, lemon slice, salt, pepper, caraway seeds, and bay leaf. Increase the heat and simmer, uncovered, until the lentils are tender, about 1 hour. If necessary, add more broth or water during the cooking process to keep the lentils at least barely covered with liquid until they are finished cooking. If there is ever too much liquid, turn up the heat to reduce the excess. Remove and discard the bay leaf.

9 oz French green lentils (see Chef's Note)

1 tbsp vegetable oil

2 slices bacon, chopped

½ cup small-dice onion

¼ cup small-dice celery

¼ cup small-dice carrot

2 garlic cloves, minced

2 tbsp tomato paste

1 qt chicken broth, plus more as needed

One ½-inch-thick lemon slice

1 tsp kosher salt, plus more as needed

4. Stir in the parsley, thyme, and lemon juice. Taste and adjust the seasoning with additional salt, pepper, and lemon juice if necessary. Serve hot or chill in the refrigerator. The ragout can be refrigerated in an airtight container for up to 2 weeks.

CHEF'S NOTE

This recipe calls for French green lentils. They are small, have a great flavor, and retain their texture when cooked. They take a good hour to cook before they are tender. If you'd like to use brown lentils in this recipe, they will cook in about 20 minutes.

½ tsp freshly cracked black pepper, plus more as needed

½ tsp caraway seeds

1 bay leaf

1 tbsp chopped flat-leaf parsley

1 tsp thyme leaves (or ¼ tsp dried thyme leaves)

1 tbsp fresh lemon juice, plus more as needed

Sauce Lamaze

MAKES 1½ CUPS SAUCE

This is a variation of a classic sauce that was created at the Warwick Hotel in New York City to be served with shrimp. It comes as a welcome relief from the more common cocktail sauce, since it will not dominate the shrimp or mask the smoke flavor as cocktail sauce can. This versatile sauce can be used as a dipping sauce for fish and other seafood as well.

1. Combine the mayonnaise, sour cream, chili sauce, lemon juice, Worcestershire sauce, relish, parsley, and salt and pepper as needed in a bowl and mix until thoroughly combined.

2. Cover the bowl and refrigerate the sauce for at least 1 hour before serving.

3. Before serving, taste and adjust the seasoning if needed. The sauce can be refrigerated in an airtight container for 1 week.

½ cup mayonnaise

½ cup sour cream

½ cup chili sauce

½ tsp fresh lemon juice

¼ tsp Worcestershire sauce

2 tbsp pickle relish

1 tbsp chopped flat-leaf parsley

Kosher salt, as needed

Freshly cracked black pepper, as needed

Tomato Sauce

This is a very simple and flavorful sauce. It can be used as is or can be embellished with cooked ground meat or sausage, mushrooms, or other vegetables. San Marzano tomatoes, which are famous for being especially flavorful, are not a particular brand, but a variety grown in specific regions of Italy using heirloom seed stock.

1. Heat the olive oil in a large saucepan over medium-high heat. Add the onions and sauté until translucent, about 6 minutes. Add the garlic and sauté until fragrant, about 1 minute.

2. Add the tomatoes and bring the sauce to a boil. Reduce the heat and simmer for 20 to 25 minutes.

3. Add the basil and simmer for 5 minutes more. Season with salt and pepper. Refrigerate the sauce in an airtight container until needed, up to 3 weeks.

3 tbsp olive oil

2 yellow onions, finely diced

8 garlic cloves, minced

One 28-oz can plus one 14.5-oz can whole San Marzano tomatoes, chopped

1 tbsp chopped basil

Kosher salt, as needed

Freshly ground pepper, as needed

CHEF'S NOTE

For a smoother texture, the sauce can be passed through a food mill or puréed in a food processor.

Chimichurri Sauce

MAKES 1 CUP SAUCE

Chimichurri sauce is the ketchup of Argentina. The country is well known for their high-quality beef, and the beef industry is a vital part of their economy. Because of this, chimichurri is generally served with beef, particularly grilled beef, but it also goes well with pork, chicken, and fish.

1. Combine the parsley and cilantro in the bowl of a food processor and pulse a few times to finely chop the herbs. Add the olive oil, vinegar, salt, black pepper, and red pepper flakes and pulse until the mixture is well combined. Add the garlic and pulse quickly to combine.

2. Transfer the sauce to a bowl and set aside for 30 minutes to allow the flavors to blend. Refrigerate in an airtight container until needed, up to 2 weeks.

CHEF'S NOTE

If you do not have a food processor, all of the dry ingredients can be chopped by hand with a knife and then combined with the wet ingredients. If desired, you can use a mortar and pestle, as that is the traditional way of making this sauce.

1 cup roughly chopped flat-leaf parsley leaves (about 1 bunch)

1 cup roughly chopped cilantro leaves (about 1 bunch)

½ cup extra-virgin olive oil

¼ cup red wine vinegar

1 tsp kosher salt

¼ tsp freshly cracked black pepper

⅛ tsp crushed red pepper flakes

2 large garlic cloves, coarsely chopped

Tomato Salsa

This is a mild salsa. If you like more heat, leave some of the ribs and seeds on the jalapeño before you dice it.

1. Combine the tomatoes, onion, cilantro, jalapeño, garlic, oil, lime juice, and salt in a large bowl.

2. Set the salsa aside for about 30 minutes before serving to allow the flavors to blend. The salsa can be refrigerated in an airtight container for up to 2 days. Bring to room temperature before serving.

CHEF'S NOTE

To make tomatillo salsa, replace the tomatoes with tomatillos.

2 cups seeded and diced fresh tomatoes (from about 1 lb)

⅓ cup diced red onion

3 tbsp chopped cilantro

2 tbsp diced jalapeño, seeds and ribs removed

1 tbsp chopped garlic

1 tbsp extra-virgin olive oil

1 tbsp fresh lime juice

½ tsp kosher salt

Pineapple Salsa

This tropical-flavored sauce is great for barbecued and grilled meats. It is particularly tasty with salmon, pork, and chicken.

1. In a bowl, combine the pineapple, cucumber, jícama, bell pepper, onion, jalapeño, cilantro, lime zest, lime juice, sesame oil, honey, and salt and pepper as needed. The finished salsa should have a sweet, sour, and slightly hot, spicy flavor. Taste it and, if necessary, adjust the seasoning with a little sugar or additional lime juice, jalapeño, or cilantro until you are happy with the balance of flavors.

2. Refrigerate the salsa for 1 hour before serving to allow the flavors to blend. Serve chilled or at room temperature. The salsa can be refrigerated in an airtight container for up to 1 week.

1¼ cups small-dice fresh pineapple

½ cup seeded and diced cucumber

⅓ cup small-dice jícama

⅓ cup small-dice red bell pepper, ribs and seeds removed

⅓ cup small-dice red onion

1 jalapeño, ribs and seeds removed, minced, plus more as needed

2 tbsp chopped cilantro, plus more as needed

1 tbsp grated lime zest

2 tbsp fresh lime juice, plus more as needed

2 tbsp sesame oil

1 tbsp honey

Kosher salt, as needed

Freshly ground black pepper, as needed

Sugar, as needed

Ajili Mojili—Hot Pepper and Garlic Sauce

MAKES 1 CUP SAUCE

This spicy sauce can be served with all meats and fish. It is particularly good with Lechón (Puerto Rican–Style Roast Suckling Pig) (page 146).

1. Place the chiles and garlic in the bowl of a food processor and pulse until smooth.

2. Transfer the chile and garlic mixture to a bowl and add the lime juice, oil, salt, and pepper. Mix well. Refrigerate in an airtight container until needed, up to 2 weeks.

CHEF'S NOTE

Using freshly squeezed lime juice makes a huge difference in the flavor of the sauce.

6 green hot chiles, seeded and chopped

¼ cup garlic, roughly chopped

½ cup fresh lime juice

½ cup olive oil

2 tsp kosher salt

½ tsp freshly cracked black pepper

Glossary

BARBECUE A long, slow cooking method in which the temperature is maintained between 225° and 250°F, and where the fire is fueled with hardwood or charcoal in a grill, pit, or smoker. To cook food by grilling it over a wood or charcoal fire; often a marinade or sauce is brushed on the item during cooking. The term also refers to meat or poultry that has been cooked in this way.

BARD To cover a naturally lean meat with slabs or strips of fat such as bacon or fatback, which baste the meat during roasting or braising. The fat is usually tied on with butcher's twine.

BOIL To cook food by fully immersing it in liquid at the boiling point (212°F).

BRAISE To cook food using a combination cooking method (see page 233) by which the meat is seared and then placed in a pot, liquid is added, and the pot is covered and placed in the oven to simmer in the 185° to 210°F range.

BRAISER A pan designed specifically for braising that usually has two handles and a tight-fitting lid. Often round or oval but may be square or rectangular. Sometimes called a rondeau.

BRINE A solution of salt, water, and seasonings used to preserve or moisten foods.

BRISKET A cut of beef from the lower forequarter, best suited for long cooking methods such as braising. Corned beef is cured beef brisket.

BROIL To cook food by means of a radiant heat source above it.

BROILER The piece of equipment used to broil foods.

BULLET SMOKER A narrow, tall smoker topped with a tight-fitting lid, which looks like a large bullet.

CARAMELIZATION The process of browning sugar in the presence of heat. The caramelization of sugar occurs between 320° and 360°F.

CARRYOVER COOKING The heat retained in cooked foods that allows them to continue cooking even after removal from the cooking medium. Especially important with roasted foods.

CERAMIC COOKER Similar to the bullet smoker in many ways, but made of ceramic material. This allows ceramic cookers to attain a much higher heat for grilling and to maintain heat with a minimum amount of opening to add fuel or smoking material.

CHARCOAL Carbonized wood scraps that are used in barbecuing methods.

COLD SMOKING A procedure used to give smoked flavor to products without cooking them.

COLLAGEN A fibrous protein found in the connective tissue of animals, used to make glue and gelatin. Collagen breaks down into gelatin when cooked in a moist environment for an extended period of time.

COMBINATION METHOD A cooking method that involves the application of both dry and moist heat to the main item (e.g., meats seared in fat, then simmered in a sauce for braising or stewing).

CURE To preserve a food by salting, smoking, pickling, and/or drying.

DIRECT HEAT A method of heat transfer in which heat waves radiate from a source (e.g., an open burner or grill) and travel directly to the item being heated with no conductor between heat source and food. Examples are grilling, broiling, and toasting. Also known as radiant heat.

DUTCH OVEN A kettle, usually of made cast iron or enameled cast iron, used for stewing and braising on the stovetop or in the oven.

ELECTRIC SMOKER A chamber that will hold several racks and will allow you to hang food in it. It also has a water pan to keep the humidity level high. An adjustable electric element that produces heat allows for an even temperature in the smoke chamber. There is an internal or external smoke generator involved, which produces the smoke for the chamber. This involves a heating element that will smolder wood sawdust, wood chips, or briquettes that are produced by the manufacturer.

FAT POCKET Fat between the seams of muscles on the side of the butt that does not contain the bone.

FOND The pan drippings remaining after sautéing or roasting food, often deglazed and used as a base for sauces or pan gravies in order to add flavor.

GRILL To cook foods by a radiant heat source placed below the food. Also, the piece of equipment on which grilling is done; it may be fueled by gas, electricity, charcoal, or wood.

GRILL PAN A skillet with ridges, which is used on the stovetop to simulate grilling.

INDIRECT HEAT A method of heat transfer in which the heat is transferred to the product by the heated air instead of the heat source.

KOSHER SALT Pure, refined salt, also known as coarse salt or pickling salt. Used for pickling because it does not contain magnesium carbonate and thus does not cloud brine solutions. It is also used to make kosher meats and poultry.

LARD Rendered pork fat; used in pastry doughs and for frying. The term also refers to inserting small strips of fatback into naturally lean meats before roasting or braising. The process, known as larding, is done using a larding needle.

MARBLING The intramuscular fat found in meat that makes it tender and juicy.

MARINADE A mixture used before cooking to flavor and moisten foods; may be liquid or dry. Liquid marinades are usually based on an acidic ingredient such as wine or vinegar; dry marinades are usually salt-based.

PAN GRAVY A sauce made by deglazing pan drippings from a roast and combining them with a roux or other starch and stock or broth.

PICKLING SPICE A mixture of herbs and spices used to season pickles. Often includes dill weed and/or seed, coriander seed, cinnamon stick, peppercorns, and bay leaves, among others.

PLATEAU A term in the barbecue world that refers to a point at which a beef brisket or pork butt will hold at a certain temperature for a period of time.

REST To allow food to sit undisturbed after roasting and before carving; this allows the juices to redistribute into the meat fibers. In yeast dough production, the stage that allows the gluten in preshaped dough to relax before the final shaping; also known as secondary fermentation.

ROAST To cook by dry heat in an oven or on a spit over a fire.

ROUX A mixture containing equal parts of flour and fat (usually butter), used to thicken liquids. Roux is cooked to varying degrees (white, blond, brown, or dark), depending on its intended use. The darker the roux, the less thickening power it has but the fuller the taste.

RUB A combination of spices and herbs applied to foods as a marinade or flavorful crust. Dry rubs are generally based upon spices. Wet rubs, sometimes known as mops, may include moist ingredients such as fresh herbs, vegetables, and fruit juice or broth, if needed, to make a pasty consistency. Rubs are absorbed into the meat to create a greater depth of flavor.

SEAR To brown the surface of food in fat over high heat in order to add flavor before finishing by another method of cooking (e.g., braising or roasting).

SEASONING Adding an ingredient to give foods a particular flavor, using salt, pepper, herbs, spices, and/or condiments.

SLOW COOKER An electric appliance used for slow cooking, also known by the trademark Crock-Pot. They have tight-fitting lids to hold in moisture. The meat cooks in liquid at a low temperature.

SLOW ROASTING A dry heat cooking method in which meat is roasted slowly in a 200° to 250°F oven.

SMOKER An enclosed area in which foods are held on racks or hooks and allowed to remain in a smoke bath at an appropriate temperature.

SMOKE POINT The temperature at which a fat begins to break down and smoke when heated.

SMOKE RING A pink or red ring around the edge of a finished barbecued product that results from a chemical reaction between nitrogen dioxide and the amino acids in the meat.

SMOKE-ROASTING A method of roasting foods in which items are placed on a rack in a pan containing wood chips that smolder, emitting smoke, when the pan is placed on the stovetop or in the oven.

SMOKING Any of several methods for preserving and flavoring foods by exposing them to smoke. Methods include cold smoking (in which smoked items are not fully cooked), hot smoking (in which the items are cooked), and smoke-roasting.

SPIT-ROAST To roast an item on a large skewer or spit over, or in front of, an open flame or other radiant heat source.

Conversions and Equivalents

Experienced home cooks have traditionally relied on pinches, dashes, and a little of this or that. They know when a food is done cooking by touch or feel. They can accomplish this feat because they have become accustomed over time to the way foods look when they are done, what their hands and fingertips can hold, how fast salt pours from their shaker, and how full their pans and bowls typically look when making a particular dish.

However, you may want to follow the measurements given in a recipe exactly the first time you make it, then make adjustments to suit your taste. If you are reading and using these recipes in a kitchen outside of the United States, you will most likely need to convert to metric measurements for weight, volume, and temperature. The unit of measure for oven temperatures in some areas also differs from those in the United States; gas marks are used instead of a Fahrenheit or Celsius temperature. The information in the following charts allows you to make a variety of conversions—pounds to kilograms, ounces to grams, cups to milliliters and liters, Fahrenheit to Celsius, and volume to weight.

USEFUL MEASURES

3 tsp = 1 tbsp
4 tbsp = ¼ cup
16 tbsp = 1 cup
1 cup = ½ pt = 8 fl oz
2 cups = 1 pt
2 pt = 1 qt
4 qt = 1 gal
1 stick butter = 8 tbsp = 4 oz = ½ cup

To convert Fahrenheit to Celsius
Subtract 32. Divide result by 9. Multiply result by 5 to get Celsius.

To convert Celsius to Fahrenheit
Multiply by 9. Divide result by 5. Add 32 to get Fahrenheit.

USEFUL TEMPERATURES

Water freezes at 32°F, 0°C.
Water boils at 212°F, 100°C.

To convert ounces and pounds to grams and kilograms

Multiply ounces by 28.35 to determine grams; divide pounds by 2.2 to determine kilograms.

To convert grams to ounces or pounds

Divide grams by 28.35 to determine ounces; divide grams by 453.59 to determine pounds.

To convert fluid ounces to milliliters

Multiply fluid ounces by 29.58 to determine milliliters.

To convert milliliters to fluid ounces

Divide milliliters by 29.58 to determine fluid ounces.

TEMPERATURE CONVERSIONS

GAS MARK	FAHRENHEIT	CELSIUS	DESCRIPTION
1	275°	135°	Very slow oven
2	300°	150°	Slow oven
3	325°	160°	Slow oven
4	350°	180°	Moderate oven
5	375°	190°	Moderate oven
6	400°	200°	Hot oven
7	450°	230°	Very hot oven
8	475°	250°	Very hot oven

WEIGHT CONVERSIONS

U.S. UNIT	METRIC UNIT (ROUNDED)
½ oz	15 g
1 oz	30 g
2 oz	55 g
3 oz	85 g
4 oz (¼ lb)	115 g

U.S. UNIT	METRIC UNIT (ROUNDED)
8 oz (½ lb)	225 g
1 lb (16 oz)	455 g
5 lb	2.25 kg
10 lb	4.5 kg

VOLUME CONVERSIONS

VOLUME MEASURE	U.S. VOLUME	METRIC (ROUNDED)
1 tsp	⅕ fl oz	5 ml
1 tbsp (3 tsp)	½ fl oz	15 ml
⅛ cup (2 tbsp)	1 fl oz	30 ml
¼ cup	2 fl oz	60 ml
½ cup	4 fl oz	120 ml
⅔ cup	5 ⅓ fl oz	160 ml
¾ cup	6 fl oz	180 ml
1 cup	8 fl oz	240 ml
¾ pt (1½ cups)	12 fl oz	360 ml
1 pt (2 cups)	16 fl oz	480 ml
1 qt (2 pt)	32 fl oz	950 ml (1 L)
1 gal (4 qt; 16 cups)	128 fl oz	3.75 L

Index

Page numbers in *italics* indicate illustrations